Peru Before Pizarro

Series edited by Paul Johnstone and Anna Ritchie

PERU
Before Pizarro

George
Bankes

PHAIDON · OXFORD

For Catherine and Mary Jane

Phaidon Press Limited, Littlegate House, St Ebbe's Street, Oxford
Published in the United States of America by E. P. Dutton, New York

First published 1977

© 1977 George Bankes

ISBN: hardback 0 7148 1784 8
        paperback 0 7148 1785 6
Library of Congress Catalog Card Number: 77–75402

Printed in Great Britain

Contents

An Indian from the coast of Peru, modelled in clay some fifteen hundred years ago.

Acknowledgements

My chief thanks are to the Amenities Committee of Brighton Borough Council for granting me permission to write this book. I am indebted to John Morley, Director of the Royal Pavilion, Art Gallery and Museums, and David Cordingly, Principal Keeper of Antiquities and Interpretation, for their encouragement and advice. My research has been greatly helped by Kent Day, Royal Ontario Museum; Tom Pozorski, Department of Anthropology at the University of Texas, Austin; Carol Mackey, Department of Anthropology at California State University, Northridge; and Elizabeth Carmichael and her staff of the Museum of Mankind. Especial thanks is due to John Barrow for his photography and to Michael Jones for drawing the map and some of the line drawings. Finally I am most grateful to my wife Catherine for her comments on my manuscript and to Sally Kington of Phaidon for her patient editorial work.

The extract on page 34 from one of Max Uhle's letters is taken from *Max Uhle, 1856–1944. A Memoir of the Father of Peruvian Archaeology* by John H. Rowe (University of California Publications in American Archaeology and Ethnology, 1954).

A temple built by the Moche and now known as the Huaca del Sol had long fallen into disrepair by the time of the Spanish conquest of Peru in the 16th century. One side then collapsed when the conquistadors diverted the Moche River to wash out potential treasure and its mud-brick structure has since been further eroded by heavy rains, especially in 1925, and by earthquakes.

Chapter I Conquest and Rediscovery

The Spanish conquest of Peru

The Spaniards not only discovered Peru but also provided the name. There are a number of stories about its origin. One is told by Garcilaso de la Vega, the son of an Inca princess and a Spanish conquistador. Garcilaso relates how, in about 1515 or 1516, a Spanish ship had just crossed the equator and was sailing close in to the shore (i.e. was very likely off the coast of what is now known as Ecuador). The Spaniards sighted an Indian fishing at the mouth of a river. They decided to capture him by having their ship sail up and down in front of him to distract his attention while four of their number landed a little further down the coast and caught him unawares. He was brought on board ship. When he had overcome his fear at the sight of the Spaniards they asked him, by means of signs and words, what the land was called. He probably did not really understand what they were asking but since he was afraid they might harm him he quickly replied by saying '*Beru*' and adding another word '*pelu*'. He may have meant that his name was Beru and that he was in the river (*pelu*). At any rate the Spaniards either took the name *Beru* and altered the B to a P or took *pelu* and altered the l to an r and obtained Peru.

Neither the Incas nor their predecessors used the name Peru. The Inca empire was known as *Tawantinsuyu* or 'The Land of the Four Quarters'. This covered an extensive area from the northern border of Colombia with Ecuador to the Maule river in central Chile, a distance of some 4,000 kilometres. However, whereas the modern republic of Peru includes a large segment of the Upper Amazon basin, relatively little of this area came within the Inca empire. Pre-Inca peoples had names for places and localities but do not seem to have had the equivalent of Tawantinsuyu.

Although the Spanish conquistadors, under the command of Francisco Pizarro and others, were responsible for the destruction of many fine pieces of Inca goldwork and brought virulent diseases which killed many of the

9

Indians, some of their number left very useful written records. Since neither the Incas nor their predecessors could write, our only written records of Inca and pre-Inca culture consist of Spanish accounts at the time of and soon after the Spanish conquest. They can be used to help archaeologists, particularly in the study of settlements and temples which feature in them.

While Atahualpa was being held prisoner by Francisco Pizarro and his men in Cajamarca he suggested to the Spaniards that they might ransack the temple of Pachacámac for gold. At Pachacámac, on the central coast of Peru, there were two temples: an Inca one dedicated to the Sun and an older, pre-Inca one. The latter had an oracle inside which was consulted from far and wide. Atahualpa suggested the looting expedition partly because he was displeased with the oracle which had advised him to make war on the Spaniards, saying that he would kill them all. Instead he had become their prisoner.

Hernando Pizarro, half-brother of Francisco, was dispatched with a small expedition of twenty horsemen (including the author Miguel de Estete) and some foot soldiers in January, 1533. They spent about fifteen days riding through the mountains after which they descended to the coastal plain and spent another week on the road before reaching Pachacámac. The distance covered between Cajamarca and Pachacámac was probably in the region of 800 kilometres.

Once at Pachacámac Hernando Pizarro demanded that the priests bring all their gold to him so that he could take it to Cajamarca. A relatively small quantity was brought. After this Hernando demanded to be taken to see the oracle of Pachacámac. Estete describes how the temple which housed this oracle was a 'place great to behold' with two 'gate-keepers' at the first doorway. Then he relates how Hernando, himself and some of the Spaniards were led through many doorways until they arrived at the 'summit' of the temple. This suggests that it was built on more than one level. At the top were 'three or four winding blind walls' after which they emerged into a small courtyard. Beyond the courtyard was the structure where the idol was housed. This structure is described as 'built of branches, with some pillars embellished with leaves of gold and silver, and on the roof some matting-like fabric to keep off the Sun, as is the custom in all the houses in that land, for as it never rains, no other cover is used'. Beyond the courtyard was a closed door, which was closely studded with coral, turquoise, crystal and other materials. Once the door was opened the Spaniards found themselves in a small dark chamber described by Estete as 'a very small cave, rough, with no carvings, and in the middle of it there was a wooden stake planted in the ground with the figure of a man badly carved and crudely shaped out of its upper part, and at the foot around it were strewn many objects of gold and silver, offerings made over a long time and half buried in the earth'. The Spaniards were disgusted by this idol and its sanctuary. They gathered together the highest ranking priests and told them that the idol and its

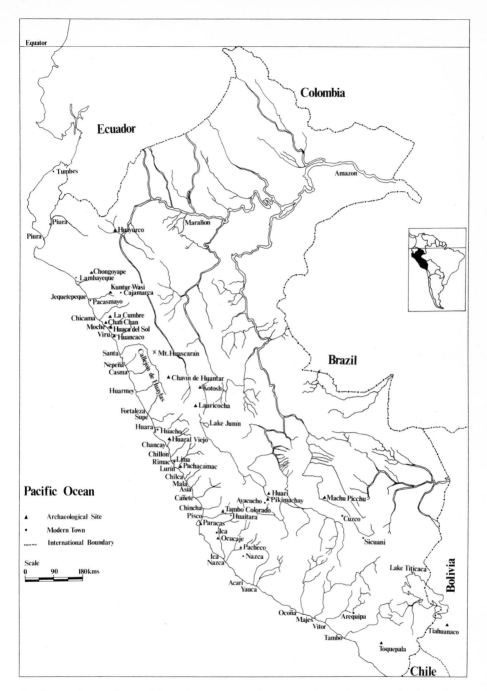

Equator

Colombia

Ecuador

Amazon

· Tumbes

Piura
Piura
▲Huayurco
Marañon

▲Chongoyape
Lambayeque
Kuntur-Wasi
·Cajamarca
Jequetepeque
·Pacasmayo
Chicama ▲ La Cumbre
▲Chan Chan
Moche ▲Huaca del Sol
Viru ▲Huancaco

Santa ×Mt.Huascarán
Nepeña
Casma ▲Chavin de Huantar
▲Kotosh
Huarmey
▲Lauricocha
Fortaleza
Supe Lake Junin
Huara ▲Huacho
Chancay ▲Huaral Viejo
Chillón
Rimac·Lima
Lurin ▲Pachacamac
Chilca
Mala
Asia ▲ Huari ·Machu Picchu
Cañete Ayacucho·Pikimachay
Chincha Tambo Colorado ·Cuzco
Pisco ·Huaitara
▲Paracas
·Ica
▲Ocucaje ·Sicuani
▲Pacheco
Ica ·Nazca
Nazca

Brazil

Callejon de Huaylas

Pacific Ocean

▲ Archaeological Site
· Modern Town
---- International Boundary

Scale
0   90   180kms

Acari
Yauca

Lake Titicaca
Bolivia

Ocoña
Majes ·Arequipa
Vitor
Tambo ▲Tiahuanaco
Toquepala

Chile

Settlement in pre-Spanish Peru. The names of some of the ancient peoples have been recorded: as, for example, Chimú or Inca, with capitals at Chan Chan and Cuzco. Others are named after the places where their cultures have been identified: often one of the coastal valleys like Moche or Nazca.

11

sanctuary would have to be torn down. Once this had been done a large cross was put in its place with due ceremony.

Estete describes the town of Pachacámac as being very large. Close to the pre-Inca temple the Incas had built a temple to the Sun. This was set on a hill and had five surrounding walls. He also noted that the town seemed to be very old, to judge from the ruined houses that it contained. In addition, much of the outer wall had fallen down. One architectural feature that Estete noted was that there were houses with terrace roofs as in Spain.

After the destruction of the oracle at Pachacámac, the town was transferred to another site by Augustinian monks in the early 1550s. When they left, their successors changed the site of the town once more to a point several kilometres inland, where it stands today.

Squier at Pachacámac

In the 1860s George Squier, United States Commissioner to Peru, travelled round the coast and mountains of Peru, visiting many archaeological sites. Unfortunately he had a mental breakdown before he could finish writing about his experiences and his book *Peru. Incidents of Travel in the Land of the Incas* had to be put together by his brother Frank. This may partly account for the rather impressionistic nature of this nineteenth-century travelogue in which some of the detailed descriptions and interpretations have to be carefully checked. However Squier was a trained surveyor and some of his work is still studied and quoted by modern students of Peruvian archaeology.

One of the sites visited by Squier was Pachacámac. He describes the ruins as 'most forbidding in aspect . . . a waste of sand, which has been drifted into and over a large portion of the buildings within the outer walls, some of which have been completely buried'. After quoting Estete's description Squier noted that the population now only consisted of a few families living in a '. . . little village still called Pachacámac'.

During his explorations of the ruins Squier was nearly attacked by a condor. On the seashore, only a few hundred yards away from the ruins of the Inca temple to the Sun, were some whale carcases with condors feeding on them. One day, while he was sketching in the ruins, a shadow suddenly fell on his drawing board. He heard a sharp report like the noise of two boards being banged together. On looking up he saw a huge condor, not more than fifteen feet above him, apparently ready to pounce. He jumped to his feet, pulled out his pistol and fired at the bird. The latter wheeled away for a few hundred yards but then returned to hover 'at a more respectable distance'. This time he took more careful aim and managed to dislodge one of the wing feathers which was 61 centimetres long. He was not troubled by that condor for the remainder of the day.

In Squier's description of the ruins there seems to be some confusion as to which building was the Inca Sun Temple and which was the temple of the

United States Commissioner, George Squier, did his own drawing of his defence against a threatening condor while he was exploring the ruins of Pachacámac.

pre-Inca oracle. He talks of one building called 'El Castillo or The Temple, which supported the shrine of Pachacámac', and 'which occupies the summit of a considerable hill, or rather headland, projecting from the somewhat elevated level behind, and rising about five hundred feet above the sea'. Several earlier writers, such as the Jesuit Bernabé Cobo in the early seventeenth century, described the Inca Temple of the Sun as being the highest one as well as that nearest the sea. The plan which Squier drew of 'El Castillo' is definitely that of the Inca Sun Temple, even though he does not specifically identify it as such.

The only Inca-type building to which Squier refers is the 'Mamacuna' situated about 2 kilometres from the ruins of 'El Castillo'. Squier noted Inca-style doorways and niches in the 'Mamacuna' (now usually known as the *Mamacona* or Nunnery). One peculiar feature of this building which he noticed was an arch made of large *adobes* (sun-dried mud-bricks) which covered a passage into the structure. Max Uhle, who worked at Pachacámac in 1896–7, pointed out that this arch dated from the Spanish period. It had been put into the place of an Inca niche, cutting it out and fitting the recess. The top was closed over with the arch. He also noted that the quality and plastering of the arch was inferior to that of the original Inca structure. Squier's description of this arch suggests that he thought it was contemporary with the original Inca building but Uhle's opinion is correct.

Squier did investigate some of the graves in the extensive cemeteries at Pachacámac. In the dry sand the bodies of the dead easily became mummified. They were usually buried in a sitting position, with the head resting on the knees. Cloth wrappings were wound round almost all the mummies. Squier points out that sometimes these mummies 'are enveloped in inner wrappings of fine cloth, and then in blankets of various colours and designs, made from the wool of the *vicuña* and *alpaca*, with ornaments of

13

In a tomb at Pachacámac Squier found the bodies of a man, a woman and three children. Under a coarse outer wrapping of braided reeds, the woman was wound in an alpaca wool blanket and a fine cotton sheet (above).

14

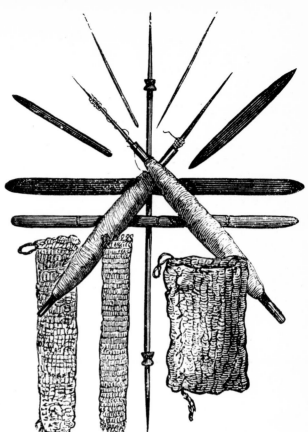

Among tools and goods buried with the family at Pachacámac were the man's fishing tackle, the woman's knitting and spinning implements (right) and a pouch (below) with her ear-rings in it and pods of raw cotton as well as some lima beans. The girl had a 'Dab' (below right) for putting on make-up. Squier drew these finds for his book of travels.

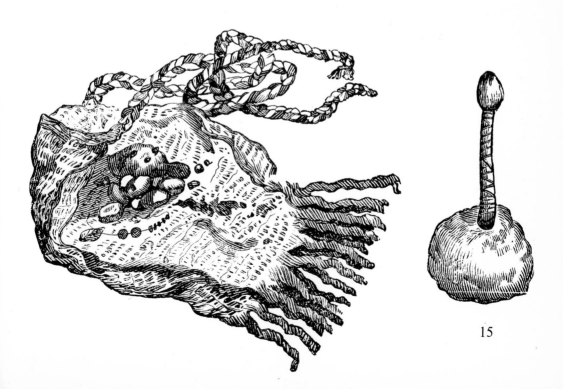

15

gold and silver on the corpse and vases of elegant design by the side'. He goes on to say that the 'interment of articles of any kind with the dead is a clear proof of a belief in a doctrine of a future state, the theory being that the articles thus buried would be useful to their possessor in another world'. Squier does not offer a date for these mummies nor does he present enough evidence, apart from one tomb, to allow an accurate estimate of their age to be made. However, since most of the burials found by later archaeologists, such as Uhle, have been of pre-Inca date, then it is likely that the age of Squier's mummies is also within the pre-Inca period. This would date them to before AD 1470, the approximate date of the Inca conquest of Pachacámac.

Perhaps Squier's most important piece of archaeological work at Pachacámac is his description of the contents of one of the tombs. The tomb he describes is from the second of three levels of graves which he found in the cemetery round the temple. It is not clear from his text whether this temple is the Inca one or that of the pre-Inca oracle. The tomb had a wall made of adobe bricks and measured about 1 metre square by 92 centimetres deep. It contained five bodies: one of a middle-aged man, another of an adult woman, a third of a girl about fourteen years old, a fourth of a boy some years younger and finally that of an infant. The infant was placed between the man and the woman while the girl was at the side of the woman and the boy at the side of the man. Squier thought that they were one family.

When he unwrapped the body of the middle-aged man Squier found a plain cotton cloth layer underneath an outer one of braided reeds. Next was a covering of finer textured cotton cloth underneath which was the well-preserved shrunken body. The hair was slightly reddish, possibly due to the nitrate in the soil, while the skin was the colour of mahogany. Wrapped in a cloth between the feet were various sizes of fishing lines, some barbed copper hooks and a few copper sinkers. Not surprisingly this evidence suggested to Squier that the man was a fisherman. In his mouth had been placed a small thin piece of copper. Squier thought this might have corresponded to the *obol* or small coin which the ancient Greeks put into the mouths of their dead as a fee for Charon, ferryman of the river Styx. Suspended by a thread round the neck of the fisherman was a pair of bronze tweezers for plucking out facial hair.

The fisherman's wife had the same coarse outer wrapping of braided reeds underneath which was a finely spun alpaca wool blanket in two colours, '. . . a soft chestnut brown and a pure white'. The design on this blanket consisted of birds set in diagonal parallel lines. Since the birds shown in Squier's illustration are quite stylized it is impossible to say exactly what they are, although they might be condors. Underneath was a fine cotton sheet with a diamond-shaped pattern and what Squier describes as '. . . representations of monkeys, which seemed to be following each other up and down stairs'.

Ceremonial knife of Chimú workmanship. Chimú metal-workers ▶
were employed by the Incas at Cuzco.

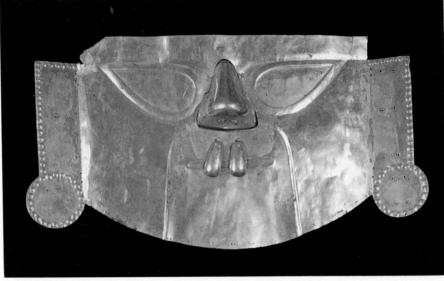

After removing the fine cotton sheet Squier came to a rather coarsely woven cotton cloth about 18 metres long which was wrapped round the woman's body. The woman's body was in a similar state of preservation to that of her husband. Her long black hair had been braided and wound in plaits round her head. Some of it was still lustrous and had not been affected as much by the salts in the soil as her husband's had been. In one hand she held a comb whose teeth were made of what Squier took to be the rays from fish fins tightly cemented and firmly bound into a piece of wood. In her other hand were the remains of a feather fan with a cane handle. The feathers, of parrots and humming-birds, were only slightly faded.

Around her neck was a triple shell necklace which seemed to have faded. In between her body and her knees, which were drawn up close to her chest, were her spinning implements and other tools. There was an old spindle about 8 inches long (20 centimetres), made from a section of *quinoa* stalk (quinoa is a high-protein grain plant that grows in the Peruvian highlands), with its lower end fitted through a round stone spindle whorl and a wooden point stuck into its upper end. This spindle would have been turned by the forefinger while the wooden point was held steady by the thumb. The spindle was half covered with spun thread that was still connected to a mass of raw cotton. Squier noted that this apparatus was much the same as that used by Indian women when he was touring Peru. The difference he noted was that the spindle whorls were made in his time from a small lime, or from a lemon or a potato rather than from stone or earthenware. One can still see Indian women using spindles like those Squier saw.

One interesting item which Squier found with the fisherman's wife was what he describes as a 'kind of wallet'. It was made of two pieces of thick cotton cloth of different colours, measuring 254 millimetres by 127. The lower end of each piece was fringed while a long braid at the upper end of each corner and the braids of both were again woven together. The two cloths had been carefully folded up and tied by the braids. Inside this 'wallet' were some lima beans, a few immature cotton pods with their husks still on, some fragments of a thin silver ornament and two little thin silver discs, 7·6 millimetres across, each pierced with a hole near the edge. Squier suggests that these last items were too small for ornaments and may have functioned as coins. However, some pre-Inca portraits, on pots, do show what look like metal discs hanging from the ears so that the discs in the wallet may have been small ear-rings. The beans had been placed under her chin and may have been to feed her, as Squier speculates, '. . . on the way to the realms of the god Pachacámac, and the silver discs to propitiate the fiends and monsters which the Indian imagination pictures as obstructing the passage of the dead from earth to heaven'.

The body of the girl had been buried in a seated position on a sort of workbox made from braided reeds with a cover hinged on one side and

◄ Chimú gold masks, both expertly made but the bottom one recently shown to be only 40% gold.

fastening on the other. It was about 46 centimetres long, 35·5 centimetres wide and 20 centimetres deep. Squier suspected that the girl had died before her mother since the items in her workbox showed a lack of finish. Some of the little strips of knitting stitches had been 'dropped' as if the girl were still learning to knit. There were two miniature spindles, weaving implements, and braids of thread of irregular thickness as well as other larger well-wound spindles with a finer and more even thread. In addition there were woven strips of cloth of various thicknesses and some in two or three colours. There were also needles, all of bone except for one of bronze. A fan, smaller than the mother's, was stored in the box. The girl had a comb as well as a little bronze knife and some other articles. Squier was slightly puzzled by finding several sections of the hollow bones of pelican (or some other large sea-bird) which contained pigments of various colours and were each carefully stopped by a wad of cotton. He thought at first that they were intended as dyes for the cotton textiles. However, he found a '. . . curious contrivance made of the finest cotton . . .' which his wife's hairdresser said was a 'Dab'. This 'Dab' was for putting the make-up contained in the hollow bones on to the girl's face.

By the side of the hollow bones containing the make-up was a small apparatus for grinding up the pigments into the necessary fine quality. A small oblong stone had a cup-shaped hollow on the upper side into which fitted a little round stone. The latter functioned as a pestle or crusher.

For a mirror the girl had a piece of iron pyrites, about half the size of an egg, with one side highly polished. She also had a little crushed gold ornament which Squier thought was intended to represent a butterfly. It was so delicate that it came to pieces when handled. In addition there was an instrument made of hard wood like that used in making nets. In Squier's opinion this girl may have helped make nets for her father.

Like her mother's, the girl's hair was plaited and braided round her forehead; around her head was also wound a band of white cloth ornamented with little silver bangles. On her arm, shrunken from being buried so long in the sand, was a thin silver bracelet. Between her feet was the dried body of a parrot, which may have come originally from one of the Upper Amazon valleys.

The only item which Squier records as being buried with the boy is a sling which was finely braided from cotton threads. This sling was bound tightly round his forehead.

The infant was a girl whose body had been placed first in alpaca wool, then wrapped in a fine cotton cloth and finally put in a braided sack of rushes, with handles or loops at each end which may have been used for carrying it. The only object found with the infant was a sea shell containing pebbles, the mouth of which had been sealed with a hard, pitch-like substance. Squier came to the conclusion that this shell was the child's rattle.

Squier recorded a temple standing high above the sea's edge at Pachacámac. It remained for Uhle to prove that it was the Inca Sun Temple (above). A house with the stumps of its roof posts still in place (right) is a survivor from AD 600–800 of the pre-Inca town whose Temple of the Oracle Uhle also identified.

Besides the six mummified bodies he found six earthenware pots of various sizes. One or two still had an encrustation of soot which had presumably come from fires over which they had been used. Each pot contained something such as peanuts or maize, and everything, except the maize, was thoroughly charred.

Squier's account of the tomb is illustrated by drawings of some of the contents such as the pottery, the 'wallet' in its folded and unfolded state, the bronze tweezers and the boy's sling. Even though he does not give a detailed plan of the tomb or an exhaustive list of its contents his description is very valuable for the information it gives on burial practices. Nobody before his time had given such a comprehensive description of an ancient Peruvian tomb. He does not mention a date but the style of the birds on the alpaca blanket, the shapes of the six pots and the position of the grave in the 'second stratum' suggests a pre-Inca date, possibly between AD 1000 and 1470.

Max Uhle

Max Uhle is often regarded as the father of Peruvian archaeology. He was the first archaeologist in Peru to apply seriously the principle of stratigraphy and understand that when layers are superimposed the upper one is later than the lower one. His most important field work was at Pachacámac where he established an archaeological sequence which he was later able to extend to many other parts of the Peruvian coast and highlands.

Uhle was born in Dresden, Germany, in 1856. His training in Germany was first of all in linguistics but soon after receiving his Ph.D. on the subject of Chinese mediaeval grammer he switched to archaeology and ethnography. While he was curator at the Dresden Museum he met Alphons Stübel and Wilhelm Reiss who had excavated a cemetery at Ancón on the Peruvian coast. The publication of the results of this excavation in German and English in 1880–87 was quite a landmark in Peruvian archaeology since it was the first descriptive report on a scientific excavation in Peru. Uhle was not only influenced by this book, entitled *The Necropolis of Ancón in Peru*, but also had personal encouragement from one of its authors, Alphons Stübel. Stübel lived in Dresden and knew Uhle well, perhaps inspiring the young museum curator to make Andean archaeology his life's work.

Uhle's field research in South America began in 1892 with a trip to Argentina and Bolivia. After this he continued to do field work in South America, with a few breaks, for over thirty years. His best work was in Bolivia and Peru between 1893 and 1910. In later years he went to Chile and Ecuador where he set up museums and conducted excavations.

His work in the museums first of Dresden and then of Berlin made Uhle familiar with the Inca and Tiahuanaco pottery styles. At the Berlin Museum he was able to study a collection of late Inca antiquities and in consequence was able to recognize Inca pieces wherever they were found. He went on to write up Stübel's notes on Tiahuanaco. Immediately he noticed that the Tiahuanaco style of sculpture differed from that of the Incas. He found statements from sixteenth-century Spaniards that Tiahuanaco was already in ruins by the time that the Incas got there from which he could infer that the Tiahuanaco style of sculpture and pottery was older than the Inca one. This knowledge served him in good stead particularly when he excavated at Pachacámac in 1896 to 1897. His work there was on the largest scale he ever undertook. His findings were promptly published in 1903 and in consequence had an immediate and lasting effect on Peruvian archaeology.

The financing of Uhle's work at Pachacámac, together with the publication that followed, was the work of the University of Pennsylvania. From 1892 to 1893 his work in Argentina and Bolivia had been sponsored by the Prussian government and the Berlin Museum. During 1893 Bastian, director of the Berlin Museum, agreed to allow the University of Pennsylvania to take over the sponsorship of Uhle's work. But it took many months to raise the money in Philadelphia to finance him and in the period between April and September of 1894 Uhle was so short of funds in La Paz that he had to borrow money to live on. Finally, early in 1895, he started work for the University of Pennsylvania.

Uhle at Pachacámac

Uhle made his headquarters for the Pachacámac excavations at the Hacienda San Pedro owned by Don Vincente Silva. He noted that the mestizos (those of mixed Spanish or Creole and Indian blood) of the modern village of Pachacámac had a similar type of face, with a long narrow chin and rather aquiline nose, to that shown on a Chimú pot illustrated by Squier.

The actual ruins of Pachacámac are situated on the north side of the Lurín Valley, near the river mouth and only about 549 metres from the Pacific Ocean. Both to the north and south of the Lurín Valley stretches the Peruvian coastal desert. Vegetation is scanty and consists of a few *tillandsia* plants which are only green in winter. Uhle thought that the coastline near the ancient town had undoubtedly changed even before the Spaniards arrived. He is not specific as to exactly how it had changed but was probably referring to various levels of shore lines left as a result of changes in sea level during the advances and retreats of the polar ice caps. He also points out that the fields between the town and the beach were sometimes inundated by heavy tides, possibly indicating that these fields were on land reclaimed from the sea.

Before he describes his excavations Uhle surveys the language and known history of Pachacámac and its people. According to Bernabé Cobo a distinct language was spoken in the valleys of Rimac (where Lima now stands) and Lurín. Cobo also noted that it was still spoken by some individuals as late as 1630. Neither Uhle nor Squier mention finding anyone still speaking it.

Uhle draws on the chronicler Garcilaso de la Vega for the history. According to Garcilaso the valleys of Lurín, Rimac, Chancay, Huacho, Supé and Huamán (Barranca) were ruled, during the period preceding the conquest of that territory by the Incas, by a chief who had his seat at Pachacámac. He, like the Inca at Cuzco, had the right to enter the temple of the chief deity although not in the same way as the high priest. The area ruled over by the chief of Pachacámac was about 192 kilometres long but really only consisted of a few narrow valleys with wide deserts in between. Garcilaso suggests that the connection between the different parts of the realm was very loose for geographical reasons. He tells of wars carried on by the rulers of Pachacámac with the Chimú and of defeats suffered by the former.

The supremacy of the ruler of Pachacámac still seems to have continued into the Inca period. Francisco Pizarro, when he founded the city of Lima in the valley of the Rimac, enumerated Rimac as part of the Pachacámac district. Uhle mentions that the names of only four of the rulers of Pachacámac were known in his day. The earliest was Kuismanqu, who surrendered to the Incas. Then came Taurichumbi, who ruled at the time of Hernando Pizarro's arrival. His name seems to have been derived from *Quechua* (the official language of the Inca empire) since '*chumpi*' in Quechua means belt and '*tarhui*', also a Quechua word, refers to a type of grain. Taurichumbi was followed by Saba who was baptized by Augustinian friars in the 1550s. Finally Luyan soon succeeded Saba since the latter did not prove subservient enough.

The name Pachacámac is used by most writers to refer specifically to the idol destroyed by Hernando Pizarro. Garcilaso calls the creator of the world Pachacámac. Since the cult of this idol was so important the Incas found it suited their purpose to identify it with their own creator to the extent of calling it *Pacha Kamaq* or 'Creator of the World'. The Inca creator god was called 'Viracocha' but Pachacámac was never referred to by this name.

According to Uhle's estimate the ruins of Pachacámac extended over an area about 4 kilometres long by half a kilometre wide. He maintained that it was still possible to distinguish a street crossing which divided the town into quarters. There is some evidence for this shown on his plan but there does not seem to have been a well planned division into four quarters.

One of the principal aims of Uhle's excavations seems to have been to locate and study the temple which housed the pre-Inca oracle. To help him in his search he used the accounts of Estete and others as a guide. Estete located the pre-Inca temple as being '. . . built against the northwest slope of the hill, on the summit of which, further to the south, the ruins of the Sun temple were to be seen'. The pre-Inca temple faced north-west and, in Uhle's opinion, probably faced the older part of the town. The temple measured about 400 feet (120 metres) long by 180 feet (54 metres) wide, covering an area of about two-thirds of an acre (0·25 hectares). It was terraced on three sides and the northern face had eight terraces, each no more than 3 feet (91.5 centimetres) high. The top formed a 'plateau' measuring 330 feet (99 metres) long by 130 feet (39 metres) wide. It had a nearly rectangular form, closely following the general outlines of the building.

On the 'plateau' on top of the structure Uhle could only trace a few details. He reckons that the shrine of the temple, torn down by Hernando Pizarro, must have been here. No evidence is presented of the actual place where the idol might have stood. The remaining area of the 'plateau' was divided by a partition wall into an eastern and western section. The eastern section measured about 170 feet (51 metres) long by 130 feet (39 metres) wide. Uhle concludes that this must have been the large hall where possibly the high priest stood and received envoys of chieftains.

Uhle's main work at the temple consisted in his discovery and interpretation of the different levels of burials in the crowded graveyard at the northern base of the temple. The cemetery measured about 750 feet (225 metres) long with a general width of 200 feet (60 metres). He estimated that there were about 30,000 burials in it. According to the chroniclers Zarate and Cieza de León, burial in front of the famous Pachacámac shrine was a privilege reserved for priests, princes and those pilgrims who could bring rich offerings to the sanctuary. However, most of the skulls were of the common coastal type that had been artificially flattened at the back in infancy. There were a few other types and these were generally found in graves close to the front walls of the temple. The small number of other skull-types indicates that relatively few people from areas other than the coast, such as the highlands, were buried here. Uhle came across little archaeological evidence to suggest that the shrine was much revered but did find marked differences of period in the contents of the cemetery. Most of the burials were made in the pre-Inca period and this concentration of pre-Inca material, together with the lack of Inca items, confirmed Uhle in his belief that this was definitely the temple of Pachacámac and was not connected with Inca worship of the Sun.

The descriptions and illustrations which Uhle gives of his excavations are rather complicated. They can be explained by referring to a simplified version of one of his cross-sections. Close to the surface of the 'New Soil' just in front of the lowest terrace of the temple of Pachacámac he found individual mummy bundles at a depth of 5 feet (152·5 centimetres). The pottery buried with them was either pure Inca or made on the coast near the time of the Inca conquest. These graves were in the form of conical or cylindrical chambers, constructed of stone or adobe. A few were roofed over with stone but the majority had a covering of cane matting or similar material. In some cases the roof was supported by a pole in the centre. Uhle describes the mummies as generally being '. . . in the shape of bales or

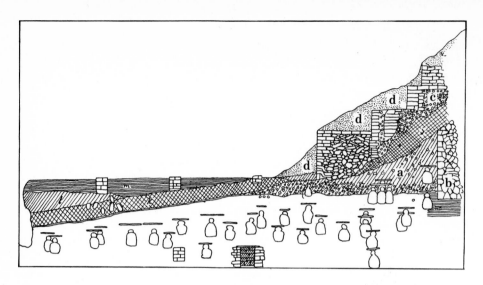

Uhle's section through the cemetery at the foot of the Temple of the Oracle at Pachacámac. Soil (a) had piled up against the lowest terrace of the first building on the site (b). A new building (c) had been put up on top of it and had itself been smothered by sand (d) by the time Uhle rediscovered it. The dead had been wrapped into bundles and buried in individual stone- or cane-roofed chambers.

packages, with a false human head attached, the face of which is carved of wood or is merely painted on a stuffed cushion, or occasionally made of burnt clay and crudely tinted'. Most of the mummies were buried facing east and the temple at the same time.

Underneath the terraces of the upper temple, but above the oldest cemetery, he found graves containing several mummies at depths ranging from $1\frac{1}{2}$ to 5 feet (46–152·5 centimetres). The pottery in these burials was painted red and black on white, had little polish and was rather crudely shaped. Uhle said that the surface of these vessels looked like whitewash with red and black designs. One pot had a conventionalized cat painted on the neck and the style of painting suggests a date of between AD 1000 and 1470. Another had a conventionalized double snouted head in what Uhle termed the 'Epigone' style—now dated to AD 800–1000. There was also some pottery which was either Chimú or Chimú-influenced with a date probably between AD 1000 and AD 1470. Thus in contrast to his finds in front of the terraces of the upper temple, the graves underneath those same terraces yielded only pre-Inca pottery and textiles.

In front of, but deeper than, the stone wall of the lower temple Uhle found a number of graves containing pre-Inca pottery. The graves were at varying depths below the original surface, ranging from one and a half to ten feet underground (46 centimetres to 3 metres). Most of the tombs contained pots in the 'Epigone' style. There was one grave, however, which contained pottery of a richer and more elaborate kind, termed 'Coastal Tiahuanaco'

26

by Uhle, and now dated to about AD 600–800. Although Uhle did not have the aid of modern techniques like radiocarbon dating he did know how to recognize the Tiahuanaco and Inca pottery styles from his museum work in Germany. He also knew that Tiahuanaco was pre-Inca from statements of sixteenth-century Spaniards that Tiahuanaco was already in ruins by the time that the Incas got there.

One find which Uhle made at the temple of Pachacámac lent further weight to his identification of it as the place where the idol had been housed. His excavations exposed a small mural which, although rather faint in its outlines, did show human figures in yellow, white, green and black painted on a red background. More uncovering of this wall revealed eight human figures arranged as if they were walking in a procession. Some of them were connected by a line, as if by a rope. Estete had referred to the temple of Pachacámac as being 'well-painted' so this mural was probably part of the original colour scheme seen by the Spaniards.

As a result of Uhle's work not only was the temple of Pachacámac identified but also evidence was found for two phases of construction. The first had a stone front wall with a cemetery in front of it. After this cemetery had been in use for a long time the front stone wall was levelled off and the original building destroyed. Above the soil of this cemetery he found fragments of adobe bricks from the destruction of the old temple. This

As was customary in many areas of ancient Peru, the dead at Pachacámac were well wrapped up with their knees drawn up to their chins. They quickly mummified in the dry ground. These particular mummy bundles, drawn by Squier, were the type later found by Uhle at the Temple of the Oracle.

debris was piled up in front of the structure to form a slope. The terraces of the later, enlarged temple were built on top of the debris of the old temple. Some of the pottery which Uhle found in graves in this debris were Chimú or Chimú-influenced types. The occurrence of these vessels led him to the conclusion that the people who had destroyed the original temple had cultural relations with the northern part of the Peruvian coast where the Chimú people lived.

The other main buildings which Uhle examined at Pachacámac were the Inca Sun Temple and the Mamacona. The latter was described by Hernando Pizarro as follows: 'Outside of it (city of Pachacámac) is another large space enclosed by walls with gates opening into the mosque. In this enclosure are the houses of the women, who are wives of the devil.' They were probably Virgins of the Sun. Basically the Mamacona consisted of a sunken courtyard around which rooms and trapezoidal niches were arranged. The roofing of all the niches was made of wooden boards bound together with ropes. These boards had been, in Uhle's time, nearly all torn out of the walls so that the general effect of the niches was destroyed. There were also traces of rooms with flat roofs.

Near the Mamacona Uhle noticed that there were fields still bearing the same name as the building. In his opinion these represented the complex of arable land set apart by the Incas for the cult of the Sun in newly conquered provinces. The produce of these fields probably fed the women who lived in the Mamacona.

The Sun Temple had been built up on a rocky hill some 250 to 300 feet high (76 to 91 metres). It was constructed in the form of an irregular trapezoid with, according to Uhle, a south-western length of 715 feet (218 metres), a north-western length of 515 feet (157 metres), a north-eastern length of 565 feet (172 metres) and a south-eastern length of 347 feet (106 metres). He notes that 'On the side facing the ocean the most delightful sea-breeze is felt all day long, making the crest of this hill a pleasant place, even on the hottest day.' The elevated nature of this structure was in keeping with Inca ideas of building their temples in a commanding position.

Uhle gives the height of the temple structure on the south-western front as 75 feet (23 metres) with a variation on the other three sides of 49 to 60 feet (15–18 metres). He postulated that the main entrance was on the north-west side where there were passageways running up to it. He thought that there was another entrance near the southern end of the north-eastern front.

The lowest terraces of the temple may have served as living quarters and stores. Uhle quotes Roman, a sixteenth-century chronicler, who says: 'Within the lower terraces were the apartments of all the servants, priests and priestesses connected with the Temple. There were rooms for the manufacture of the Temple decorations, cellars and storerooms for the liquors (vinos), and living and slaughtered animals and birds were kept here for the sacrifices. There were sacristies where might be seen hangings of wool and cotton of the finest colour and texture, and so the entire edifice was excellently arranged (estava muy clara todo) and everything easily to be found.'

In the upper part of the Temple Uhle noted Inca-style niches. These were, however, plain and square and probably represented a more primitive type than the trapezoidal ones of the Mamacona. He emphasizes that the Temple as a whole represented a blending of Cuzco Inca and Coastal architectural styles and had more in common with the architecture of Pachacámac than with that of the Mamacona.

On the lowest terrace of the south-western front of the Sun Temple Uhle found and excavated an almost pure Inca cemetery. The pottery he found in it was almost pure Cuzco Inca in style while the textiles were of highland types. Coastal foods like *yucca* (also known in English as manioc and cassava), *camote* (sweet potato) and *lúcuma* (a fruit) were absent from the tombs. Instead there were offerings of *t'unta* (a preparation of white potatoes), quince, beans of *aji* (cayenne pepper) strung on twine, and *coca* (a tropical shrub whose leaves are a source of cocaine). About two per cent of the objects found in this cemetery were of coastal type. All the people interred were women and children. There were complete sets of women's clothes and numerous 'topos'—large bronze pins for fastening clothes. Uhle reckons that all these people died of strangulation. He cites examples of vertebrae being found in a distorted position beneath the back of the lower jaw-base. Presumably these were sacrificial victims from the highlands. Human victims sacrificed by the Incas were usually strangled with a cord, had their throats cut or had their hearts cut out and offered, still beating, to the deity.

Uhle at Moche

In 1897 Uhle left Peru for the United States to write up his report on Pachacámac at Philadelphia. He was there from 1897 to 1899. During this period he met his future wife, Charlotte Grosse, daughter of Dr. Johannes Grosse and Luise Wulkop. Miss Grosse was brought into frequent contact with Uhle since she had the job of translating his German manuscript on Pachacámac. They were finally married in Philadelphia in 1903.

Before his marriage Uhle returned again to Peru, this time with a different sponsor. Dr. William Pepper, Uhle's chief patron at the University of Pennsylvania, died in 1899. However Mrs. Phoebe Hearst, a close friend of Dr. Pepper's, came to his aid with an offer to finance a new Peruvian expedition for him. In 1900 she transferred the official sponsorship of the expedition to the University of California who also began to receive Uhle's finds.

In June, 1899, he sailed for Peru again. For some time he had wanted to work on the north coast and in particular in the valley of Trujillo.

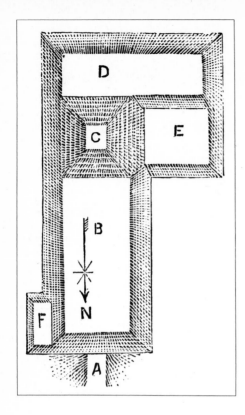

Squier's conjectural plan of the Huaca del Sol, the Temple of the Sun at Moche, has been corroborated by recent archaeological work. A ramp (A) gave access to five platforms, the highest (C) standing about 41 metres above the valley floor. The sides of the mound were steeply terraced and have now been badly eroded both by the weather and by looters. Most of one platform (E) has vanished altogether.

In the valley of Trujillo Uhle visited Chan Chan, the Chimú capital, the pyramids of Moche and other sites. He decided to concentrate his work at Moche since this site seemed to have more chance of yielding earlier material than the others. The Moche ruins are located about 6·5 kilometres south-east of Trujillo between the Moche River and the Cerro Blanco, a conical peak about 370 metres high. At the foot of this peak lies the Huaca de la Luna (a name given to it by the Spaniards). This structure is made of adobe bricks and has a main platform measuring about 75 metres by 60 metres and is about 23 metres above the plain. It probably served as a temple platform. About 495 metres to the west is the Huaca del Sol, a large pyramid built of adobe bricks (another structure named by the Spaniards). The Sol has a maximum height of about 41 metres above the valley floor. Its total length is some 240 metres with a maximum width of about 120 metres. It was probably a temple.

In November, 1899, Uhle found an undisturbed cemetery containing what he called Proto-Chimú pottery (now known as Moche or Mochica) at the west foot of the Huaca de la Luna. He excavated thirty-two graves and published illustrations of two tombs which showed them to have had a lining of adobe bricks. The pottery evidence from this cemetery suggested to Uhle that the Huaca de la Luna dated exclusively to the Proto-Chimú period. He

The summit of the Huaca del Sol
(above). This temple mound, and
another, the Huaca de la Luna, lie on
the southern margin of the cultivated
land in the Moche Valley. Here too was
one of the valley's burial grounds,
where Uhle took his only photograph of
a Moche grave (right), complete with
pots and provisions for the after-life.

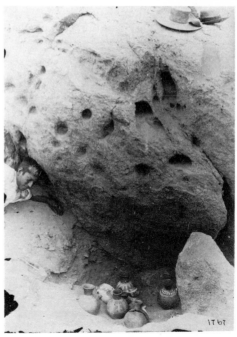

31

catalogued all the specimens according to the tombs from which they came with the result that modern scholars can easily see what pots and other items came from each grave. To this day this cemetery remains the largest one for the Moche culture to have such accurate records. Unfortunately Uhle only published a preliminary paper on this work but the contents of the tombs have been largely published by later scholars, particularly Kroeber.

On the platform at the south end of the Huaca del Sol Uhle found the remains of a cemetery which contained some Proto-Chimú potsherds and also sherds of the Tiahuanaco and 'Epigone' type as found at Pachacámac. In addition he found several intact graves sunk into the pyramid terraces or walled in with adobes. The pots in these graves were mainly blackware with elaborate relief designs. The tombs had been filled with soil containing sherds from the adjacent Tiahuanaco cemetery. Uhle concluded that these graves with blackware pottery represented the final phase of the cemetery's use. These finds led him to think that, whereas the Luna was a Proto-Chimú structure in both construction and period of use, the Sol, although originally built in Proto-Chimú times, had continued in use during the Tiahuanaco era and in at least one subsequent period.

Other work carried out by Uhle at Moche included the excavation of a cemetery, about 49 metres south of the Huaca del Sol, containing some blackware Late Chimú vessels and some Inca.

The excavation of the cemetery at the west foot of the Huaca de la Luna continued until February, 1900. After that Uhle had to spend a month packing up the finds from his excavations. In April he went to the highlands to study archaeological sites round Huamachuco in order to find out whether they related to the great archaeological sites on the coast. He worked at sites like Marca Huamachuco and Viracochapampa, measuring and describing the ruins and making collections of stone sculpture, pottery and metal artifacts both by excavation and by purchase.

Uhle in south Peru

In July, 1900, Uhle returned to Lima where he spent two months seeing to expedition business and also making short visits to archaeological sites near Lima and in the Lurín Valley. In September he went down the south coast to Chincha where he worked until the early part of December. Next he went to the Ica Valley and worked there until May, 1901. While there he concentrated on the Hacienda Ocucaje where he was the first to identify the Early Nazca pottery style, mainly known hitherto from a few isolated specimens in the Berlin Museum. Near Ica he found later material including rich tombs of the Inca period containing carved wood, jewellery and some gold and silver.

After leaving Ica Uhle spent a month and a half in the Pisco Valley where his main work consisted in measuring and photographing the well-preserved Inca palace of Tambo Colorado. Then he followed one of the principal Inca roads up into the highlands to Huaitará where he found that the village church consisted of little more than a facade added to a converted Inca building. According to John Rowe, a modern specialist on the Incas, this church is the only well-preserved example of such re-use known anywhere in Peru. After returning from Huaitará in October Uhle went back to Lima and sailed for San Francisco.

Uhle's final work

On the University of California campus at Berkeley Mrs. Hearst had built a temporary store to house, among other things, the collections sent back by Uhle that were eventually intended for the projected university museum. Uhle worked in this building but preferred to live in San Francisco and commute to Berkeley. Apart from excavating a huge mound of shells at Emeryville, near Berkeley, and giving some lectures, his main task was to unpack and study his collections and write reports. He wrote the text of the latter in German. In addition he had hundreds of photographs and drawings made for his illustrations. Specialists at Berkeley identified his materials and shells.

The reports were finished by early October in 1903 in the form of seven manuscripts. In June of that year he married Charlotte Grosse on the strength of a new three-year contract from Mrs. Hearst for an expedition to Peru. It was decided to allow Mrs. Uhle to translate her husband's manuscripts. Unfortunately she only completed the translation of two out of the seven, and the manuscripts were never sent back to California although their return was repeatedly requested. One reason for this situation may have been that Uhle was unhappy about the publication format. The University of California intended Uhle's reports to be issued in three memoirs in a quarto format. He much preferred the folio form of his Pachacámac report since the larger page size made it possible to print the photographs on a bigger scale. At any rate Uhle kept the manuscripts, plans, ink drawings and original field notes with him. At his death they passed to the Latein Amerikanische Bibliothek in Berlin. The photographs remained in Berkeley together with the collections, his field catalogues and some long and informative letters.

In November, 1903 the Uhles sailed from San Francisco for Peru under the sponsorship of the University of California. They reached Callao, the port for Lima, on the 10th of December. To give his wife a chance to adjust to life in Peru, Uhle decided to conduct his first excavations at Ancón, a fashionable summer resort on the coast just north of Lima. From January to May in 1904 he carried out quite extensive excavations. In addition to the Ancón cemetery, long-known for the contents of its graves, there was a small shell mound on the south side of the town. Nobody had explored this mound before. In it Uhle found unpainted black pottery decorated with incised and some other related designs. He dated this early Ancón pottery to the beginning of his Peruvian sequence because he regarded it as primitive in the evolutionary sense. In doing this he was proved correct by later investigators. He had in fact made a very important discovery since this Early Ancón pottery was the first archaeological evidence for what was later called the Chavín or Early Horizon. The objects made and used by these early Ancón people were few and not very elaborate. They did not have the elaborate architecture and stone carving which is found at Chavín itself. Probably the local economic conditions at Ancón did not allow for a very rich culture, with the result that the material remains were but a provincial version of Chavín.

As there was an outbreak of plague in Lima when the Uhles finished at Ancón, they took a boat direct to Chancay, a few miles to the north, instead of returning to the capital. They worked in the Chancay Valley from May to September and dug at five different sites. Uhle discovered two new pottery styles which were later known as Interlocking and White-on-Red. He decided that both these styles were pre-Tiahuanaco and that Interlocking was earlier than White-on-Red. Unfortunately he did not clearly present the evidence for these conclusions. In 1941–2 Gordon Willey found further stratigraphic evidence for White-on-Red being earlier than Interlocking. This was the only serious error in dating that Uhle made in his work in Peru.

A crucial event now happened in Uhle's life. He had a serious accident while working at one of his Chancay sites, Huaral Viejo. He fell head first into a trench three metres deep and severely sprained his neck. In a letter to Professor Putnam at Berkeley, dated November the 3rd, 1904, he says: 'But though I fell head foremost about 10 feet deep and some of my neck was sprained I recovered soon under the care of Mrs. Uhle and my field work was in no way interrupted.' In spite of this statement John Rowe, in his study of Max Uhle's life, has pointed out that the quality of Uhle's work showed a distinct falling off after the Chancay accident. His reports became less de-tailed and more infrequent. He also gave more attention to interpretation at the expense of description.

In September the Uhles moved north to the Supé Valley. After some reconnaissance they settled down to work at the site of Chimú Capac on the Hacienda San Nicolas. Here they found remains of Tiahuanaco-period influence. The collection they made is notable for the preservation of textiles and wooden objects. Uhle found two more early Ancón type sites near Puerto de Supé. The notes he supplied on the work at Supé are less clear and detailed than those on the previous collections. Nowhere does he say when the Supé work was finished although it was probably about the end of the year.

In 1904 Uhle heard that Mrs. Hearst wanted to cut back her archaeological work. He was told by a letter of October 8th that he should

Peru's coastal valleys are irrigated by mountain river water. This ▶
part of the south coast is entirely without rain.

plan to finish his field work in time to get back to San Francisco and write up his field work. He agreed to these proposals but felt that the future looked very insecure since he might find himself unemployed in San Francisco in 1906. This problem of Uhle's future was solved by a proposal from the Peruvian government that he should undertake to found a national archaeological museum in Lima. Not only was the government giving support for the museum but it was also interested in the protection of ancient sites. Uhle liked Peru and felt that there were endless opportunities for field work. He accepted the job in Lima without hesitation. Mrs. Hearst willingly released him from the remainder of his contract with her and terminated it on the 31st of December, 1905.

On the 1st of January, 1906 Uhle took up his post in the new museum. The collections had to be made almost from scratch since about all there was to start with was the famous Raimondi monolith from Chavín, a rectangular, carved stone, measuring about 1·83 metres high by 76 centimetres wide, which was taken from Chavín to Lima in the early 1870s on the instigation of Antonio Raimondi, an Italian naturalist and geographer. The new museum was housed on the second floor of the former Palacio de la Exposición which needed quite a lot of remodelling for its new purpose. By the time of the official opening on the 29th of July, 1906 Uhle had assembled an impressive collection from the valley of Lima. He had also bought a collection from the Trujillo area. In addition there was some ethnographic material, mostly from the Aguarina, a sub-tribe of the Jívaro Indians.

Uhle remained the head of the national museum in Lima until 1912. During this time he found that his administrative duties allowed him less time than before in which he could do his field work. He made some trips into the highlands. In 1907 he was in Cuzco and excavated some tombs at Qhatan near Urubamba, where he found the first examples of the Early Inca pottery style.

In 1910 the Uhles visited Chile on an official excursion of the 7th International Congress of Americanists held in Buenos Aires. It was probably during this visit that the ground was laid for an invitation to come to Santiago, which Uhle accepted in 1911. Nobody knows the exact reasons for this move. The Uhles seemed quite happy in Lima with their lovely house on the Avenida de la Magdalena and he specifically says that his wife was most unhappy to leave. In spite of all this they left Peru. There may have been some problem at the Lima Museum but this does not appear to have been recorded by Uhle. He spent the next four years, 1912–15, organizing an archaeological museum in Santiago. After this move to Chile Uhle did not return to Peru to carry out any significant field work. In recognition of his work in Peru he received, on his eightieth birthday in 1936, the Orden del Sol (Order of the Sun), rank of commander, from the Peruvian government. He eventually died in Germany in 1944, aged 88.

◄ *The upper part of a coastal valley in Peru, its steep sides terraced to win more farming land.*

Max Uhle (next page, bottom), working in South America at the turn of the century, was the first to set the evidence for life in ancient Peru in any chronoligical order, sorting out levels of occupation at archaeological sites and coordinating them with known art styles, especially in pottery. His excavations, at which he sometimes employed professional grave-robbers, were meticulous by 19th-century standards (above), and his chronology was immediately effective at a number of places including the Chancay Valley where this little pottery doll was found (left).

The divided eyes of the god on a pot from Pacheco in the Nazca Valley (above) characterize what Max Uhle (right) termed a coastal Tiahuanaco style. Work on existing material in the Berlin Museum, as well as on his own archaeological finds in Peru, allowed him to place this second in his four-part sequence of ancient Peruvian art styles that culminated with the Inca influence.

The significance of Uhle's work

Uhle was a man of medium height, thickset, with a large bushy moustache and dark hair. The few pictures available suggest that he wore glasses as early as 1900. He seems to have been proud, slightly touchy but at the same time a rather shy person. His letters give the impression that he did not make friends easily and few of them were intimate.

The significance of Uhle's work, particularly at Pachacámac, was realized in his own day. Marie Wright, in her book *The Old and New Peru*, wrote in 1908 that 'It was while excavating these ruins (Pachacámac) a few years ago that Dr. Uhle made the discoveries which laid the foundation for a new classification of Peruvian antiquities, in accordance with the evidence of successive periods of culture.' She goes on to point out that prior to Uhle's work all Peruvian antiquities in the museums of North America and Europe were exhibited with hardly any indication of their origin.

For his day Uhle was ahead of his contemporaries in the Americas in that he realized the importance of chronology. He summed this up by saying: 'In Americanist studies, the first thing that had to be done was to introduce the idea of time, to get people to admit that types could change.' In his thinking he was probably influenced by Flinders Petrie's studies of ancient Egyptian pottery styles. Uhle's particular contribution was in setting up a relative chronology for the ancient Peruvian art styles, especially as depicted on pottery. The method used throughout his work in Peru was that of seriation of styles (i.e. their arrangement in an order). He started this before he left the Berlin Museum where he was able, on the basis of the museum's collections and written evidence about Tiahuanaco, to work out that the Tiahuanaco style of sculpture was older than the Inca one. In his field work in Peru he only found one clear case of stratigraphy—at Pachacámac—and that was the superposition of graves.

Uhle's excavations along the Peruvian coast led him to put forward a chronological scheme for Peruvian archaeology. He had a four-period sequence: early regional styles (such as Proto-Chimú), Tiahuanaco-influenced styles (such as 'Coastal Tiahuanaco'), late regional styles (like Late Chimú) and finally Inca influence. This chronology was effective at a number of places along the Peruvian coast such as the Rimac, Chancay and Moche valleys. It made use of the principle of 'horizons' (periods of widespread cultural and, sometimes, political unification) which were in this case those of Tiahuanaco and the Incas. In the main, Uhle's scheme has withstood the test of seventy years of subsequent research and has only been modified by the discovery of earlier cultures and horizons.

Chapter II Environment

When archaeologists talk about Peru before the Spanish conquest they are usually referring to the archaeological remains found on the coast of Peru and in the highlands, including that part of the Bolivian uplands round lake Titicaca. The modern republic of Peru includes quite a large area of the Upper Amazon basin which has relatively few archaeological remains as compared with the highlands and the coast. It is situated on the west coast of South America and lies within the tropics, approximately between four and eight degrees south.

There is a great range in the type of environment in Peru. Almost all the coast consists of a desert which in most years receives no proper rainfall. The traveller going east from the coastal desert first has to climb the dry, barren western slopes of the Andes but then usually finds himself descending into a well-watered valley. As he continues further east his next experience, once out of the green valley, may be of crossing a cold, barren plateau and of negotiating passes, or even a tunnel, through high, snow-covered peaks. Once on the eastern slopes of the Andes he will notice the vegetation becoming more abundant until he reaches the lush growths of the tropical forests. This means that someone who goes from the coastal desert to the highland valleys and plateaux, often over 3,000 metres, has to be careful to acclimatize himself. The air at 3,000 metres contains less oxygen than it does at or near sea-level, so that the coastal dweller finds he cannot move very quickly in the mountains. The Spaniards discovered that the Indians they took from coastal Peru to work in mines in the highlands had a very high death rate, partly because they were not given enough time to become acclimatized. Indians in the mountains find that their large chests, well suited to the thin air of the highlands, soon clog up with bronchitis and other chest diseases when they move down to the coast.

Natural disasters are frequent in the Peruvian highlands. In particular, mountain slopes are rendered unstable by the climate, rock structure, earth

41

movements and erosion. There is little vegetation to hold the earth and rocks on the mountain slopes, especially in dry areas at high altitudes, erosion by rivers and glaciers has caused the sides of valleys to become over-steepened and landslides are common during the rainy season from December to March. Earthquakes are another prime cause of landslides and Peru can expect an average of eight major ones every century. The biggest earthquake in recent years, in May, 1970, caused an avalanche of ice and rock to fall from a glacier on Huascarán, Peru's highest mountain (6,662 metres), burying almost all the town of Yungay, part of the village of Ranrahirca (already rebuilt after the avalanche of 1962) and ten small hamlets. All that was left of the centre of Yungay were a few palm trees which stood round what had been the main square. The rest of the town was covered by a deposit of mud and rocks about 3 metres deep. At least 10,000 people were killed. The inhabitants of this area, mainly Indians, have developed a fatalistic acceptance of disasters like this after several thousand years of experience.

The Pacific

The Pacific Ocean has been, and still is, an important source of food and has also exerted a strong influence on the climate of coastal Peru. Along the coast, flowing northwards, is a cool current which is popularly known as the Humboldt Current, after the German geographer and antiquarian, Alexander von Humboldt, who discovered it in the nineteenth century. It contains a large amount of plankton (a collective term of organisms that live suspended in the sea) which provides a constantly renewed source of food for bigger forms of marine life, particularly for the fish of which there are large numbers. In pre-Spanish times fish were caught with hooks and lines and a wide variety of nets. These were operated either from the beach or by men mounted on inflated skins or small rafts made of bundles of reeds lashed together. Probably the most numerous fish caught were anchovies (all about 10 to 13 centimetres long) for use as food and fertilizer. Cormorants, gulls and pelicans fed on the anchovies. The birds' droppings, deposited on rocky parts of the seashore and on some small islands just off the coast, decomposed to form guano, a manure used both in antiquity and today as a fertilizer. Other sea-life attracted by the food supply of the Humboldt Current includes sea lions, dogfish, sea snails, mussels and clams.

The cold waters of the Humboldt Current cool the prevailing south-westerly winds that pass over it and on to the land. Since they have been cooled they carry little moisture from evaporation; and what moisture there is does not produce rain over the land. Instead, the combination of cold air and warm land tends to produce fogs during about six months of the year, usually from May to October, and this period is generally known as the winter. The temperature along this coast does not have great daily or annual

Islands off the coast of Peru (below) are white with the droppings of hundreds of thousands of birds that are attracted by a mass of fish in the cool waters of the Humboldt Current. Decomposed droppings form the guano which is used now, as it was in ancient times, to fertilize coastal valleys like that of the Nazca (above).

43

fluctuations. The average annual temperature in Lima is about 18°C while the minimum temperature is about 13°C and the maximum 26°C.

Periodically this current fails and warm waters, known as '*El Niño*' (Spanish for 'The Child'), move in from the north, some brought by the Equatorial Countercurrent, others flowing out of the Gulf of Guayquil. The change in water temperature leads to quite heavy rainfall on the coast and increased rain in the highlands: the anchovies move away from the coast and large numbers of sea birds starve. These heavy rains on the coast tend to be very damaging since most buildings are of adobes, easily eroded by water, and have flat or slightly sloping roofs which are not very waterproof. As recently as 1972 heavy rains on parts of the north coast after an incursion of these warmer waters cut off the town of Chiclayo.

The coast

The desert coast of Peru in places consists of a plain over thirty kilometres wide; at other points the mountains come right down to the seashore. In many areas there are extensive stretches of sand dunes which are constantly shifting under the force of prevailing winds and sea breezes; there are also rock deserts covered with boulders and small stones. Except for the fogs almost all of the coast is very dry; and this means that much ordinarily perishable archaeological material such as basketry, cloth and wooden objects is well preserved. The desert is crossed by numerous short rivers, mainly seasonal in their flow. The smaller ones run dry or have a much reduced flow from May to November but the larger ones, mainly on the north coast, have water in them all the year round. During the rainy season in the mountains, December to March, almost all the rivers are full and some of them flood low-lying areas. In their upper courses they run through narrow gorges while some of them have deltas forming in the lower valleys where the flow has been reduced by the extraction of water for irrigation. Originally the river valleys were wooded with trees like the *algarroba* (a South American acacia) but they are now intensively farmed with cotton and sugar as the principal crops. In antiquity these rivers provided vital water supplies for irrigation with maize and cotton being the most important crops.

Between the valleys there are rocky spurs and large areas of sand hills with dunes still in the process of being formed in many places. In pre-Spanish times communication between these valleys was difficult and in consequence each tended to develop its own cultural identity. This became especially true after settlement moved inland instead of just being concentrated in fishing villages on the coast.

The winter fogs on the coast produce areas of vegetation known as *lomas* where grasses, small shrubs and other plants grow. The plants are particularly sensitive to the amount of moisture in the air so that, for example, if there are several very damp years, the lomas will expand in size especially along the lower edges. The animals found there include snails, lizards, foxes and sometimes a deer which has come down from the highlands to graze. Clumps of *mesquites* (a common name for a type of spiny shrub or small tree found in dry areas) grow on the south coast and in the far northern provinces where the water-table is high enough. Both the lomas and the mesquites were probably more extensive in antiquity. Vegetation found in the desert areas includes varieties of cacti (some of which grow to heights of 4·5 metres and more), a plant called tillandsia that takes its water supply from the air rather than the soil and shrubs like *zapote*, sometimes used as a fuel in antiquity.

On most parts of the coast breezes blow, quite strongly at times, during the middle of the day. First thing in the morning the air is usually quite still but as the day goes on the land warms up and the air above it heats up and rises. The cool air over the sea moves inland to replace the warm, rising air and this movement is the sea breeze. When these breezes blow over sandy areas they make travel on foot uncomfortable, with particles of sand getting in the eyes, in folds of the skin and into clothes.

The highlands

The highlands of Peru are part of the Andean chain which runs down the west side of South America. The Peruvian Andes are high, the highest mountain being over 6,600 metres, and rugged. They are divided by several major rivers into parallel chains such as the Cordillera Negra (literally 'Black Mountain Range') and Cordillera Blanca (literally 'White Mountain Range') along either side of the Callejón de Huaylas, an enclosed valley with Huascarán on the east side. Most of the rivers flow eastwards into the Amazon basin. There are about six areas in the highlands which appear to have supported substantial pre-Spanish populations, including the large basins round Cajamarca, the valleys and areas of flat land round Cuzco and the Bolivian plateau south of lake Titicaca. They all have fertile, well-watered soils capable of producing sufficient good crops for a large population; and in addition most of them are surrounded by a high plateau area or *puna*, covered with grasses and low bushes which served (and still do serve) as pasture areas for llamas and alpacas. The puna is inhabited to altitudes of 4,500 metres and higher.

The climate in the mountains divides into two main periods, a rainy season from December to March and a dry one for the remainder of the year. Sometimes the rains begin in November and last into April.

On the eastern slopes of the Andes is a zone of transition, known as the *montaña*, between the mountains and the tropical forest: it is heavily forested and the upper parts are generally shrouded in mist. The combination of intense rains and steep mountain slopes makes it a

45

The puna (above) is a high, grass-covered plateau lying between ranges of the Andes that run the length of Peru. The montaña (left), a steep wet zone on the eastern slopes of the Andes, plunges down to the headwaters of the Amazon.

dangerous area, unsuitable for growing crops or raising animals, although several important archaeological sites have been found there.

The tropical forest

From the foot of the eastern slopes of the Andes stretches the South American tropical rain forest or *selva*. Here a thick, rich, vegetation cover makes land travel difficult and may well be one of the reasons why the Incas and their predecessors never penetrated far inland. The whole area is crossed by slow, meandering rivers and streams which often change course. The traditional way of life of the tropical-forest Indian is based on hunting, fishing and 'slash-and-burn' agriculture. This form of agriculture involves cutting down and then burning a small patch of forest in which crops like *manioc* are planted. When the soil in one clearing is exhausted it is left to recover its fertility while a new patch of forest is burned down and planted.

The Peruvian Indians

The inhabitants of pre-Spanish Peru were all of American Indian stock and of the same race as the so-called 'Red Indians' of North America. The Peruvian Indians were (and are) short and stocky, with short, medium-to-broad heads, fairly short faces and moderately broad noses. The Indians of the highlands tended to have slightly narrower heads than those of the coast. Some of the ancient pottery of the coastal peoples, particularly the Moche, shows a range of racial characteristics extending from those with marked Mongoloid facial features to others with Negroid elements. These different types were probably the result of natural variations within the population rather than of immigration from outside. The present-day Indians, numbering at least six million out of a total population in Peru of over fourteen million, have brown or coppery skins, dark eyes and straight black hair. Originally the ancestors of these Indians came from north-west Asia and many have an oriental type 'slant' eye. Like most American Indians a high proportion of the Peruvian ones have the blood group O.

Some physical adaptation has occurred to cope with the high altitudes at which many of the Peruvian Indians live. With the thin air of the highlands containing little oxygen, large lungs are necessary, accommodated in deep barrel-type chests. In addition these Andean Indians have more blood, a higher count of red corpuscles and therefore more haemoglobin, which leads to a more rapid and efficient distribution of oxygen in the body tissues. The increase in haemoglobin is not an inherited characteristic since the Indians who move down to the coast become acclimatized through the reduction of red corpuscles. Non-Indians who move up to the highlands find that their blood gradually increases its oxygen-carrying capacity. The fully acclimatized highland Indian can be just as active, for example in performing energetic dances, as his coastal counterpart.

Archaeological evidence, especially from cemeteries, has shown that in pre-Spanish times many Indian children had their heads purposely deformed while they were still babies. This process was carried out by applying pressure with boards and straps, probably when the baby was asleep, so that when the infant grew up it would have an excessively long head, a perfectly round one or even a short or high one.

Trepanning, the surgical removal of a piece of the skull by cutting, scraping or drilling, was widely practised and the patients had a survival rate estimated at sixty per cent. The use of clubs in warfare meant many a crushed skull and the Indian surgeons may have believed that trepanning would relieve the pressure of the crushed skull on the brain. One example has been found of a piece of gold plate being used to fill the hole formed by the cut-out bone.

Before the Inca conquest of Peru in the fifteenth century the country was divided into a number of small groups each with its own language. For example the Chimú people on the north coast seem to have spoken a language later referred to as *Yunca* by the Incas. The Incas imposed their own language—usually referred to as Quechua—which they had borrowed from a neighbouring tribe. There is some evidence that Quechua was quite widely spoken in the highlands of Peru some 200 years before the Inca conquest. The Spaniards found it easier to teach Christianity to the Indians in Quechua than to instruct them first in Spanish. As a result of this policy the area in which Quechua was spoken was extended after the Spanish conquest. In central and southern Peru Quechua is still extensively used. In the Bolivian highlands and on the Peruvian side of lake Titicaca Aymara is still spoken. None of these languages was written down until the Spaniards came. Even today the Indians may learn to read and write Spanish but can soon forget these skills if they find they have no use for them. Today Spanish is the official language of Peru.

Crops

Most of the plants grown in pre-Spanish Peru were indigenous to the area; potatoes, maize and cotton were the most important ones. The potato was probably domesticated from wild examples somewhere along the Andean chain. Recent excavations in the Ayacucho area have suggested that maize may have been independently domesticated in the highlands of Peru by about 4000 BC. Also plant remains of domesticated cotton have been found near Ayacucho dating to about 4000 BC.

The type of plant grown varied with the altitude. In the highest mountain valleys potatoes, quinoa, *oca*, *ulluco* and *anu* (all root crops) were grown. These same plants grew in lower highland valleys together with

48

maize, squash (a kind of gourd), chili peppers, amaranth and lúcuma (a fruit). In the montaña there was cultivation of maize, manioc, tobacco and coca, whose leaves were (and still are) chewed along with lime as a drug by the Indians. In the coastal valleys maize, beans, peanuts, sweet potatoes, pineapple, avocado, *chirimoya* (a fruit) and chili peppers were among the cultivated plants. Almost all the plants that were grown in the highlands, except for those adapted to the high altitudes, were grown on the coast.

Animals

Both wild and domestic animals played an economic and, in some cases, a religious or mythological role, in the life of the Indians. Wild animals most frequently encountered on the coast are lizards, foxes and field owls but none of these is found in large numbers. Lizards were caught and eaten while foxes and owls tended to feature in mythology and religion. In the highlands there were *guanaco* and vicuña, Andean deer, puma, a mountain lion, and *viscacha*, a large edible rodent. Animals of the montaña included jaguars, peccaries (a kind of wild pig), tapirs, monkeys and boa constrictors. The feline, sometimes identified as a puma and sometimes as a jaguar, was an important motif in the art of ancient Peru.

Domestic animals included the dog and the muscovy duck, both of which were found outside the Andean area as well as in it. The Inca dog was a medium-sized breed with short hair and short legs; it served as pet, scavenger and hunting dog for some of the pre-Inca peoples. The muscovy, a large black, white and red duck, was reared for its meat.

The most important animals, both wild and domestic, were the American members of the camel family, namely the domesticated llama and alpaca and the guanaco and vicuña, both of which existed only in the wild state. The guanaco is usually considered to be the wild ancestor of the llama and lived throughout the central and southern highlands of Peru and in larger numbers in Argentina and Chile. The home of the vicuña was and still is the high puna. Both guanaco and vicuña were hunted in ancient times, the former for its meat and the latter for its fine wool.

Alpacas were reared exclusively for their wool. Llama wool is rather inferior so they were used as pack animals and occasionally for their meat. Llamas will carry about 45 kilos on a day's journey of 19 kilometres or so without any problem but will not take heavier loads, such as adults, over such a distance. In fact if a llama feels that it has been overloaded it is quite likely to refuse to move and to spit at the person who has put the excessive load on its back. Both llamas and alpacas were used as sacrifices in religious ceremonies. Large numbers of their bones have been found in ancient refuse heaps on the coast and evidence for the use of alpaca wool has been found there. This suggests that herds of these animals were kept in the area just as small herds of them are successfully bred there today. Studies of bones from

Four American members of the camel family native to Peru have long played a central part in the daily life of the Peruvian Indian. The guanaco, wild ancestor of the llama, was hunted in ancient times for its meat. The vicuña's fine wool has always been prized though that of the alpaca (bottom left) has been more commonly used. The llama (centre) is the pack animal. Natural home of them all are the grasslands of the puna, where their shepherding (above) is still one of the Indians' main livelihoods.

A llama with a pack on its back, portrayed by a Moche potter (above), has the short neck and slight build of a coastal breed. Another Moche animal (right) is shown carrying both pack and man, a thing it will usually refuse to do, unless perhaps it has been forced to take them both across a river.

coastal sites and depictions of llamas on modelled pots from the north coast suggest that there may have been a coastal breed of llama, slightly smaller than its highland counterpart. Today no llamas are found on much of the coast but this is probably due to the competition of animals introduced from Europe by the Spaniards. The donkey carries bigger loads than the llama and coastal Peruvians prefer beef to eat and sheep's wool to wear.

From quite early times, from about 2500 BC on the north-central coast, domesticated guinea-pigs were kept in houses. These would have been fed leftovers and scraps from the table and finally eaten. They are still reared by the highland Indians who, along with some of the coastal dwellers, consider them a delicacy. The wild guinea-pig of Peru is probably the ancestor of the domesticated one.

Chapter III Dating Ancient Peru

Archaeology

In succession to Uhle a great deal of exploring and collecting in Peru was carried out by Julio C. Tello, a man of Peruvian Indian stock from the highlands. He became such a popular and legendary figure that in the most far flung parts of the highlands the local savants preface their discoveries by saying: 'These ruins are totally unknown, not even Tello came to see them.' His most important contribution to Peruvian archaeology was his recognition of the significance and early date of the 'Chavín Culture'—a widespread cult and art style now generally known as the Chavín or Early Horizon. Tello was engaged for a while in a controversy with Uhle about the origin of Peruvian cultures: Uhle maintaining that their origin lay mainly in the Mexican area while Tello believed that they came from the Peruvian Andes. It was Tello who reorganized the National Museum of Anthropology in Lima after Uhle had left. Unfortunately he died in 1947 before much of his detailed work had been published, and it was left to the University of San Marcos, Lima, to edit his expedition notes and diaries.

In the 1930s Wendell Bennett, an American archaeologist, conducted excavations in various parts of Peru and also in highland Bolivia, especially at Tiahuanaco. Between 1941 and 1943 the Institute for Andean Research, based in the United States, conducted field work in Peru and, in particular, on the central coast where two American archaeologists, Duncan Strong and Gordon Willey, continued Uhle's work at Pachacámac. After Strong had returned to the United States Willey went on to excavate at Ancón and Supe, again sites where Uhle had worked, and increased the state of knowledge about the Chavín horizon on the central coast.

In 1946 a very comprehensive archaeological project was carried out in the Virú Valley on the north coast under the auspices of the Institute for Andean Research with the collaboration of the Peruvian Institute de Estudios Etnológicos (Institute of Ethnological Studies) and supervised by

Luis Valcárcel and Jorge Muelle. It was to survey the archaeology, human geography and ethnology of the Virú Valley from earliest times to the present day. For the first time a whole valley would be systematically surveyed with the aim of producing a complete picture of its archaeology. The most important result was probably Willey's history of the valley's settlement patterns in which he traced the history of human settlements in relation to such factors as their geographical environments, population growth, development of irrigation systems and relationships with neighbouring valleys. Before this Peruvian archaeology had largely consisted of working out pottery chronologies and excavating at a few selected sites.

Since the Virú Valley Project and particularly since 1955, a great amount of archaeological work has been carried out in Peru by Peruvian, North American, European and Japanese archaeologists. In particular, knowledge about the period before pottery was used, generally known as the Preceramic Period, has been much increased for both the coast and the highlands.

An archaeological chronology

One of the principal aims of archaeological research in Peru during the last eighty years has been to construct a chronological scheme for man's occupation from the earliest times to the Spanish conquest. Up until about 1965 a number of such schemes were in use but since then one, originally proposed by John H. Rowe and then elaborated on by Edward P. Lanning, has beeen generally accepted. Rowe's scheme of archaeological time periods was originally devised for the pottery-using cultures of Peru. It was based on interpretation of developing pottery styles as well as stratigraphy and radiocarbon dates from the Ica Valley on the south coast; and from there it was extended to other areas by comparing styles and radiocarbon dates. During the last ten years or so a great deal of work has been carried out on cultures which existed before the invention and use of pottery so that this chronological scheme has been extended back in time to include the earliest evidence of man in Peru.

Rowe originally set up his chronology by working backwards from the Inca conquest of Peru, the approximate date of which was known from Spanish records, concentrating in particular on the Ica Valley which was absorbed into the Inca empire in AD 1476. He designated the period from 1476 to the Spanish conquest in 1534 as the Late Horizon, characterized by Inca dominance of the whole of highland and coastal Peru from the present-day border of Colombia with Ecuador to the Maule River in central Chile.

Before the Inca empire came into existence there is archaeological evidence and some hint in the Spanish documents that a number of states and kingdoms existed, like that of the Chimú on the north coast. These had

Date	Period	North Peru	Central Peru	South Peru
1534				
1476	LATE HORIZON	Inca empire	Inca empire	Inca empire
1000	LATE INTERMEDIATE PERIOD	Chimú kingdom	Chancay	Ica
600	MIDDLE HORIZON	Influence from central coast and highlands	Pachacámac Huari Conchopata	Pacheco Tiahuanaco
		Moche Recuay	Beginnings of Pachacámac	Nazca
200	EARLY INTERMEDIATE PERIOD			
		Cerro Blanco Chavín influences	Chavín influences mainly on the coast	Paracas Necropolis
900	EARLY HORIZON	Chavín		Paracas Cavernas
1800	INITIAL PERIOD	Kotosh		
		Huaca Prieta	El Paraiso	
2500	PRECERAMIC PERIOD VI	Culebras		
			Chilca	Cabezas Largas
		Lauricocha Caves		
			Yacht Club	
4200	PRECERAMIC PERIOD V		Pampa	
		Lauricocha Caves		
6000	PRECERAMIC PERIOD IV			
		Lauricocha Caves		
8000	PRECERAMIC PERIOD III			
9500	PRECERAMIC PERIOD II	La Cumbre		
12,000	PRECERAMIC PERIOD I		Red Zone	
			Pikimachay Cave (17,650 BC)	
		NORTH PERU	**CENTRAL PERU**	**SOUTH PERU**

AD / BC

When and where the ancient cultures flourished in Peru.

characteristic art styles, especially in pottery and textiles, and their capitals included some large cities. This era, lasting roughly from AD 1000 to 1476 is referred to as the Late Intermediate Period.

From about AD 600 to 1000 the art styles of the cities of Huari and Tiahuanaco were spread through much of the Peruvian area. The main evidence for this spread comes from pottery and, to a lesser extent, from textiles. The period is known as the Middle Horizon.

From approximately 200 BC to AD 600 regional cultures flourished such as the Moche, whose hallmark was fine modelled pottery, and the Nazca, whose speciality was polychrome painted pottery. This is known as the Early Intermediate Period.

The Early Horizon, from about 900 to 200 BC was the period when the Chavín art style and its immediate derivatives dominated much of north Peru. This style is not represented everywhere in Peru.

Pottery appears for the first time in the Peruvian archaeological sequence between about 1800 and 900 BC. This so-called Initial Period has been considered as the time when a distinctive Peruvian cultural tradition emerged with such features as large occupation sites and notable public or ceremonial constructions. The end of the Initial Period is marked by the appearance of the Chavín art style.

Lanning has subdivided the Preceramic Period into six stages, I–VI, which are principally based on his work in the Chillón Valley on the central coast. He sees his Preceramic VI period, from 2500 to 1800 BC, as the time when agriculture and a sedentary life were adopted along much of the coast and in part of the highlands. Populations increased and maize cultivation appeared on the coast. But even with the adoption of agriculture seafood still formed a substantial part of the diet of coastal peoples.

In Preceramic V, from about 4200 to 2500 BC, the climate was getting drier and the area of lomas fog vegetation on the coast was shrinking towards its present size. A possible result of this was that the coastal peoples were spending more time in lower valley and sea-shore camps, deriving much of their food from the sea. These people had fishing gear and their sites have yielded the remains of domesticated plants including chili peppers and, towards the end of the period, cotton.

In the period from 6000 to 4200 BC, Preceramic IV, the inhabitants of the highlands were hunting Andean deer and guanaco with projectiles (probably throwing-spears) which had well-made stone points shaped like willow leaves. They probably lived in high caves, at altitudes over 4,500 metres, in the summer time and followed the herds down to the valleys at the onset of winter. On the coast the people developed a pattern of seasonally shifting between plant-gathering camps on the lomas vegetation and temporary, fishing settlements on the shore. The lomas vegetation would tend to dry up in the summer when the sea fogs were absent, and this would make the sea-shore a more viable place from which to look for food.

56

Preceramic Period III, from about 8000 to 6000 BC, seems to have been a time when the hunting of animals like deer was the main economic activity. Human skulls dating to this period have been found in the earliest level at the Lauricocha caves in the Callejón de Huaylas. In the area round Ancón, between the Chillón and Chancay Valleys, people were living in camp sites where the lomas fog vegetation provided seeds and root plants to eat.

From about 9500 to 8000 BC, Preceramic Period II, stone chopping tools, worked on both faces, were being made in the Chillón Valley. In the Ayacucho area of the central highlands the inhabitants at about this time appear to have been nomadic hunters, whose food included animals now extinct such as types of deer and possibly of horse. They made stone points shaped like fish tails, which presumably would have fitted on to the end of throwing spears.

The earliest men in Peru

The first of Lanning's Preceramic Periods has an end date of 9500 BC but as yet there is some doubt about when it began. Before going into this problem some explanation is needed of how the first men got to Peru and whence they came.

So far the only evidence from Peru and elsewhere in the Americas suggests that man came from north-west Asia as *homo sapiens* and that the land knew no forms of man such as earlier have been found in parts of Africa, Europe and Asia. The exact date of his arrival in the Americas is as yet a matter of debate and probably will never be known, but archaeological evidence, making use of radiocarbon dates, shows that he was definitely in Mexico by 18,000 BC and could have been there by 38,000 BC. He had crossed from north-west Asia to North America via the Bering Strait, a land bridge, not a channel of water, during the last ice age, when the sea-level was lower.

The first men almost certainly arrived in what is now Peru from the north, probably coming down the west side of South America from Panama. They could have come either through the Andes or along the coast where the sea-level would have been 18 tc 24 metres lower during the last ice age than it is today and the isthmus of Panama wider. Also during the last ice age the climate and vegetation of areas such as the west coast of Panama and Colombia, which today are inhospitable tropical mangrove swamps, could well have been more favourable to migrants. One authority has suggested that there was a savannah or open grassy plain in this coastal region.

The earliest evidence for man's occupation of Peru has been found in the central highlands, in the area round Ayacucho. Excavations in 1969–70 by the Ayacucho Archaeological-Botanical Project directed by Richard S. MacNeish in a cave called Pikimachay (which can roughly be translated from the Quechua as 'drunken flea') produced bones of extinct animals, including sloth, some of which seemed to have been worked by man. In the lower levels of the cave these bones were associated with a number of pieces of stone which may or may not have been made and used by men. A radiocarbon date of 17,650 ± 3000 BC was obtained from a sloth bone but whether humans were living in the cave at this time is questionable. Also a number of archaeologists have expressed doubts about the reliability of radiocarbon dates obtained from bone. Certainly there is more definite evidence for man-made stone tools such as scrapers and choppers in the period from about 14,000 to 11,000 BC. MacNeish originally claimed that the earliest signs of man's activity in the Ayacucho area dated to 21,000 BC but this is not widely accepted at present, though it is possible that man was in Peru at that date, especially as definite evidence for the earliest men in Mexico dates from 18,000 BC and possibly from 38,000 BC. MacNeish suggests that the climate of the Ayacucho area was cooler and wetter in the period from 14,000 to 11,000 BC than it is today and that there was forest vegetation near Pikimachay cave.

The earliest sign of man on the coast of Peru is still a matter of debate amongst archaeologists. In the early 1960s, in the Chillón Valley, just north of Lima, Lanning found remains of stone workshops whose surface is littered with debris from the manufacture of stone tools and weapons. The earliest date he ascribed to some of the tools found, which included steep-edged scraping and boring tools, is 12,000–10,000 BC, a date based on his estimate of the geological age of a hard reddish soil in which these tools were found. Lanning reckoned that this soil, which he called the Red Zone, had been built up during a rainy period towards the end of the last ice age. Recently, however, a Peruvian archaeologist, Rosa Fung Pineda, and several geologists have examined this site again and their findings suggest that the Red Zone was laid down under climatic conditions like those of today, marked by warm summers and cool damp winters. Therefore Lanning's date of 12,000 to 10,000 BC could be too early. The camps of these early coastal dwellers were situated in the valleys a little way from the hillsides where the workshops and quarries were located. The size of population groups was probably quite small, perhaps a few families.

These two sets of evidence show that as yet the approximate date of man's arrival in Peru is uncertain. However the evidence from the Ayacucho area suggests that he was certainly there by about 11,000 BC and may well have been in residence before then, but confirmation of this awaits more reliable archaeological evidence.

Naming the ancient cultures

Anyone who looks at the chronological tables of books on Peruvian archaeology published since 1945 will find that in some cases a number of different names is used for what is effectively the same culture. For example the name 'Moche' is more generally accepted now, as it is the name of the

The earliest signs of man in Peru have been found in caves in a valley in the Andes near Ayacucho (above). The ancient peoples' later skills are openly apparent from such buildings as the Huaca el Brujo (below), though its side is now agape from recent 'mining' for mud-bricks.

locality where this culture was centred, whereas thirty years ago *Mochica* was used, based on the vague supposition that the Moche people spoke a language called Mochica. In fact the language that the ancient Moche spoke was probably Yunca, and Mochica was a name coined by a Peruvian amateur archaeologist, Rafael Larco Hoyle. Most Peruvians still talk about the Mochica culture, mainly because the term was invented by a Peruvian, while the majority of North American and European scholars use Moche. Generally there is no problem with peoples like the Inca and Chimú since we have absolute proof from written Spanish sources that these names were applied to definite cultures by their people. As a general rule ancient Peruvian cultures are referred to by an ethnic or linguistic name if one is known to exist but, if not, then they are usually referred to by the name of the place where their culture was first identified.

Recognizing the ancient sites

Archaeological sites in Peru can be loosely classified into living sites, both temporary and permanent, cemeteries, hilltop fortresses, agricultural field systems and *huacas*. Huaca is a word derived from the Quechua *Wak'a* meaning a 'shrine' and in Inca times it was used to refer to places or objects with supernatural powers. Nowadays it describes any ancient mound whether it is just a pyramid used as a worshipping platform, such as the Huaca del Sol, or an accumulation of the remains of several centuries of human occupation, such as the Huaca Prieta. It is not always easy to classify a site in one single category since there can be some overlap, especially where the use has changed over time, as for example in the case of the Huaca del Sol where a cemetery has been found on one section. Agricultural field systems can take the form of hillside terraces or small irrigated plots on the valley floor. The seasonally occupied camps of the hunters and gatherers who first settled in Peru are examples of temporary living sites. These people had to move around after wild game or after plants which only ripened during certain seasons. In contrast were the permanent urban settlements which became possible only when a secure and stable food supply was available from agriculture and fishing. Definite concentrated cemeteries, generally set apart from living sites, really only became a feature in the period after 2500 BC, from Preceramic Period VI onwards. Hilltop fortresses mainly date from the Early Intermediate Period onwards. In addition to this classification there are a number of sites which are listed as 'temples', religious structures which may or may not have living quarters attached.

The size of settlements in ancient Peru ranged from single households to cities of probably more than 50,000 inhabitants. Some settlements were agglutinated, that is to say that most or all of the houses were built close together and the boundaries of the settlement were fairly clear. At other times houses were spaced out in a dispersed pattern.

60

Chapter IV   **Economic Life**

Hunting

The first mammals that were hunted for food in Peru probably included some which are now extinct. In the period from about 10,000 to 8000 BC the north coast of Peru was a grassland where groves of trees could be found. In this sort of environment mastodons, wild horses and cameloids (probably ancestors of the llama and alpaca) lived. Mastodons were elephant-like in appearance but were more heavily built and had long prominent upper tusks which grew parallel to each other. The legs were short, massive and pillar-like and the body was covered with long reddish-brown hair.

In 1969–70 on the north side of the Moche Valley, at La Cumbre, the bones of both mastodon and horse were found close to a number of stone tools, including heads for projectiles, probably throwing-spears, and scraping implements. The base of one projectile point was found close to rib fragments of a mastodon but it was impossible to say whether it had in fact been used to kill or wound the animal. Ancient deposits of river silt suggest that the part of La Cumbre where the mastodon and horse bones were found was a quagmire at the time that the animals died. If this was the case they were perhaps driven into the mud and then speared as they struggled to escape. Evidence for this method of hunting mammoths has been found in central Mexico. It is quite likely that the men who made and used the stone tools found at La Cumbre hunted and ate both mastodon and horse in the period from about 10,000 to 8000 BC (dates obtained from radiocarbon determinations on mastodon bones). For Paul Ossa, excavator of the La Cumbre site, the way in which the mastodon bones had been broken up suggested human activity. After the death of the mastodon and horse their carcases may have been butchered by the hunters and the meat divided up.

There have been occasional finds of mastodon remains on the central and south coast and these animals may have lived there but there is no firm evidence that they were hunted for food.

Painted at some time between 8000 and 6000 BC on a cave wall in south Peru are, among other things (far left), a llama-like animal with a long neck and a horned, deer-like beast. Hunting them are men whose weapons are either clubs or slings. Stone spearheads are also known from this early date (right) while a Chavín man of about 1000 BC carries a spear thrower as well as his spears.

In the highlands recent excavations in the Ayacucho area have suggested that sloth and ancestral forms of deer were being hunted as early as 20,000 BC. The sloth was probably the ground sloth, the largest of which is reckoned to have been the size of a small elephant. It is not clear from the archaeological evidence how the animal was hunted but since it was neither fast moving nor carnivorous it could have been cornered and killed with stones. In deposits dating from between 14,000 and 11,000 BC a sloth rib-bone was found which had been made into a knife. Other animal bones found at archaeological sites in the Ayacucho area included horse, ancestors of the modern llama, and possibly mastodon. It is likely that when these animals were being hunted, from 20,000 to 11,000 BC, grass and trees grew more freely in that area than they do today. In the period from about 8800 to 7800 BC forms of deer that are now extinct and possibly of horse seem to have been hunted in the Ayacucho region with the aid of stone fish-tail shaped points which were probably originally fixed to throwing-spears. Once killed, these animals would have been butchered with the aid of stone cutting and scraping tools.

In the Lauricocha caves, Callejón de Huaylas, the bones of llama and deer have been found associated with leaf-shaped stone points dating to about 7500 BC. The men who hunted these animals probably used throwing-spears with stone heads. The wooden shafts of these spears would have long since decayed. In the period from 6000 to 3000 BC the Lauricocha people appear to have cut up deer and other meat with a neatly made stone knife which had a specially made scraping edge on its butt. Therefore the knife could be used both to cut up meat and to scrape down hides. After 3000

A Moche seal hunt on the Pacific coast in the early centuries AD. Seals were killed for their meat as well as their skins.

BC the size of stone points found at Lauricocha gets noticeably smaller, which may indicate that they were used for arrows rather than spears. At the same time many more bone tools were being made. The excavations at Lauricocha suggested that at first, probably before 6000 BC, the meat was eaten raw but that later on it was cooked over a fire. Once the bones had been gnawed they were just thrown on the floor of the cave where they were found by the excavators in 1958 and 1959.

While the inhabitants of the Lauricocha caves depended primarily on hunting for their food, their contemporaries on the coast tended to regard meat, principally that of deer and guanaco, as a secondary food source, their diet otherwise consisting mainly of seed and root plants. Deer and guanaco on the central coast grazed on the lomas vegetation and were hunted with the aid of stone-tipped spears, probably hurled with the help of spear throwers (a spear thrower is a piece of wood with a raised notch at one end against which the base of the spear rests and which gives extra impetus when the spear is flung from it). These coastal dwellers also hunted birds for their meat.

After about 2500 BC deer hunting seems to have become relatively unimportant on the coast. But the most vivid picture of hunting methods on

A deer would not have been everyday fare in the Middle Horizon times between AD 600 and 1000 when this model was made; farming had overtaken hunting as a means of subsistence by then.

65

the north coast is provided by painted and modelled pots made by the Moche people from about 300 to 600 AD. Most of the scenes on these vessels show deer being killed with spears and clubs. Sometimes they were killed after having been driven into nets while at other times they were tracked and run down on foot, occasionally with the aid of dogs. The men who are shown killing the deer are elaborately dressed, complete with feather head-dresses, and were probably warriors and/or noblemen. Excavations in the domestic rubbish left by the Moche in the Santa Valley produced no deer bones however, while further north, in the Virú and Moche Valleys, only a few were found amongst the food remains. Therefore it seems that deer hunting was perhaps only a minority activity, possibly reserved for the nobility, and producing only a small quantity of meat for the Moche.

Besides deer, the Moche used a blowgun to shoot birds, and bird bones, especially those of the sea species, have been found in their domestic refuse. Seals and sea lions were killed with clubs, most likely for food but possibly also for their skins. Small quantities of seal and sea lion bones have been found amongst Moche food remains. Lizards, quite often depicted on pottery, may well have been trapped for food in the same way as they have been caught in this century on parts of the north coast. A long roll of matting is placed on its side, like a fence, across a field and the lizards are driven towards it where they are trapped. Lizard meat tastes rather like chicken.

Hunting in the Inca empire was only of minor importance. All the hunting grounds belonged to the emperor and nobody could use them without either his permission or that of his governor. Licences were granted at certain seasons or when there was a need for limited quantities of meat or wool due to shortages. The wild herds of deer, guanaco and vicuña were kept in hunting grounds in each province of the empire and people in one province were not allowed to hunt or interfere with animals in another. Deer and guanaco were killed for their meat while vicuñas were always taken alive and shorn, as their fine fleece was more valuable than their meat. It was always forbidden to kill female animals. The main hunting weapons were slings, small *bolas* (an illustration of a bolas used in late Inca times shows that it consisted of two stone balls attached by slender ropes to a third rope with which the whole was hurled like a sling) and clubs, which were used to kill animals that had been cornered. A rectangular net on two poles was used for catching birds, which were captured mainly for their feathers but were also sacrificed before the army went to war. Pests such as foxes, pumas and bears were killed with clubs.

Periodically the Inca emperor or one of his governors would organize a great public hunt to thin out the game in the reserve, increase the meat supply, amuse the people and provide sport for the nobility. In the mid-1530s Manco Inca held an imperial hunt in Francisco Pizarro's honour. About 10,000 Indians formed a ring, with beaters spaced at intervals, round an area 48 to 97 kilometres in circumference. They moved towards the

Reed canoes were in use in pre-Inca times in Peru (left) as they are today (below). Here one man pushes off from the shore while the other holds the boat steady with his paddle. The ancient coastal peoples appear to have taken full advantage of the fact that it is only off Peru that the fish-laden Humboldt Current sweeps close in to the South American coast.

67

centre, forming several concentric rings as their circle grew smaller, and drove all the animals in the area before them. When the circle was small enough specially picked hunters, probably nobles, entered it and killed over 11,000 animals, allowing the remainder to be freed. The meat was dried in the sun to preserve it. Another method, used for guanaco and vicuñas, was to build fences and drive the animals into a gorge.

Gathering

The gathering of plants for food was almost certainly habitual from earliest times both in the highlands and on the coast of Peru. Plant gathering always seems to have been of secondary importance to hunting for the early inhabitants of the highlands such as the Lauricocha people. In contrast their contemporaries on the coast, from about 8000 to 2500 BC, seem to have regarded seed and root plants from the fog vegetation or lomas as a primary source of food. Wild seeds were gathered and ground in mortars or on rough milling stones. Wild potatoes were among the available root plants. In addition, large land snails were collected from the lomas. By about 6000 BC grinding tools were becoming more numerous, possibly indicating an increased reliance on flour made from wild seeds. Lanning suggests that the lomas areas were largely abandoned as places to live and as a source of gathered plants by about 2500 BC. After that date fishing and, later, agriculture became the most important methods of obtaining food on the coast.

Although plant gathering became very unimportant as a source of food after 2500 BC both on the coast and in the highlands, land snails still seem to have been collected and eaten on the coast, especially by the Moche people. Snail-collecting expeditions on mountain slopes are depicted on painted and modelled Moche pottery of the period 300 to 600 AD. In the domestic refuse of a Moche house, located between the Chicama and Moche Valleys, the shells of nearly 400 land snails were found by the author during excavations in 1970. Archaeological evidence found by the Peruvian archaeologist, Dr Jiménez Borja, on the central coast suggests that in antiquity these snails were first placed in a special pen and then fed on maize to purge them of grit and fatten them up for eating. It is possible that there was such a pen in the Moche house. The snails appear during the winter season on the mountain slopes when the air is moist due to the sea fogs. The modern inhabitants of the village of Moche and other settlements in the area still collect snails and cook them by steaming.

Fishing

The most abundant and important source of fish in Peru has always been the waters of the Humboldt Current and the diet of the coastal dwellers

Some of the finest Inca terracing was built to extend the farming ▶
land to feed the mountain garrison of Machu Picchu.

throughout Peru's history has included fish and other sea foods. In the mountains freshwater fishing appears to have only been a minor activity and catches were, and still are, small.

The early inhabitants of the lomas on the central coast did some fishing but only on a small scale. However, later on, by about 3500 BC, fishing was becoming more important on the central coast. Excavations in a refuse deposit in the lower Chilca Valley, dated by a series of radiocarbon dates from 3600 to 2500 BC, showed that much of the diet consisted of seafood which ranged from fish to sea lion. Another site, known as the Yacht Club, overlooking the Bay of Ancón also, had extensive remains of seafood thus indicating that it was the main basis of the diet. Lanning suggests that these two sites were only occupied during the summer and that in the winter the inhabitants returned to the lomas where they lived by gathering and hunting. Remains of cotton fishing nets were found at both sites. At the Yacht Club site mussel-shell fish hooks and simple stone sinkers were found attached to fishing lines. In contrast the Chilca site yielded composite sinker-hooks (stone sinkers with bone barbs attached) which look like specimens that have been found on the coast of Chile far to the south.

A few miles from Ancón there is a site known as Pampa on a rocky point overlooking what was, according to Lanning, a shallow bay until nearly the time of Christ. The lower and earlier levels of the site contained mussel and clam shells (gathered from the bottom of the shallow bay), bones of fish, sea lions and shore birds, as well as large quantities of squash (a type of gourd), rinds and seeds. The upper levels have no squash remains but contain many shells and the bones of both fish and animals. This suggests that, while the inhabitants of this site, who seem to have occupied it between 4000 and 3000 BC, started as both farmers and fishermen, they gradually stopped farming and lived almost entirely off seafood. The fishing lines they used had mussel-shell hooks and simple stone sinkers similar to those found at the Yacht Club site. The Pampa site seems to have been a permanent camp which was reoccupied each summer until nearly 2 metres of refuse had built up.

In spite of the differences between Yacht Club and Pampa the evidence from all the sea-shore sites suggests that by about 2500 BC fishing, shellfishing and hunting sea lions and birds had become the most usual way of obtaining food for the inhabitants of the central coast of Peru. On the north coast at this time fishing also seems to have been a common practice but it was done with nets, with fish-hooks being hardly used at all at Huaca Prieta on the beach at the mouth of the Chicama Valley or Huaca Negra de Guañape at the mouth of the Virú Valley.

During the Early Intermediate Period, from about 200 BC to AD 600, shore fishermen continued to live in villages, many of which are still occupied today. But by this time such villages do not appear to have catered just for their own needs but also to have acted as suppliers of protein to the valleys. There is some evidence, such as the construction of fish-drying

◀ *The foot-ploughs, the woman's clod-breaker and the terrace walls are all based on Inca farming practice.*

terraces at Ventanilla and Ancón, that fishing had become industrialized and now served as only one of several food sources. However, fishing still seems to have been considered an important part of the economy since some of the fishing villages, such as Playa Grande, were protected by hilltop fortresses.

Painted and modelled pottery made by the Moche tells us that a wide range of fish was caught, from anchovies to sharks. In fishing scenes something resembling the modern casting net is depicted as well as a circular net with a handle, probably a dip net. Moche fishermen also seem to have used a harpoon. Some pots have painted scenes or modelling which suggest that rafts may have been used for fishing. These are shown with one and more earthenware jars on them and there is at least one modelled pot showing two men aboard so the rafts must have been quite large. The men wield paddles which may have consisted of a flattened piece of split cane like those used today at Huanchaco. It is very probable that their boats were like those known today as *caballitos del mar* ('little horses of the sea'). The caballito is about 3 metres long and is made of four tapering cylindrical bundles of *totora* reeds tied together to form a pointed bow and a square stern where there is a small cockpit in which the single occupant sits or kneels. Nowadays caballitos are used for surf riding but are occasionally employed by fishermen for small-net fishing, line fishing and crab-catching close inshore, especially along the coast between Huanchaco and Moche.

Excavations in Moche domestic refuse have yielded fish bones along with considerable quantities of sea shells, mainly from shellfish, and a few crab bones. One Moche house, located between the Moche and Chicama valleys, yielded nearly 1,000 sea shells, all from shellfish, which would have been obtained from the sea-shore some 11 kilometres away. Some of these, especially the *donax*, may well have been eaten in soups just as they are today in the same area.

The only place where fishing seems to have been important in the highlands was at lake Titicaca. Here the Uru, when they became subjects of the Incas, were allowed to pay their tribute in fish and were granted fishing rights in return. The Aymara made several kinds of boat, known as *balsa*, from which they fished. The Aymara people, who still live round lake Titicaca, made both small, one-man reed boats (2·4 to 3·7 metres long) and large ones (4·5 to 6·1 metres long) with a sail. In shallow water the small one was propelled by a person standing up and pushing with a pole shaped like a fork-handled sculling oar; in deep water it was used like a paddle from a sitting or kneeling position. These small boats are still in use on lake Titicaca. The large craft had a mast of two poles in the form of an inverted V and a wooden hook at the top for raising and lowering the sail. In these sailing balsas the fork-handled sculling oar was kept in the stern. Tacking was probably unknown so that the sail would only have been used in a following wind. Reed mats on a bent-pole frame provided shelter. The boats were anchored with large stones, perforated or grooved round the middle for a rope.

The first agriculture

When and where farming first began in Peru is not yet precisely known. But it does seem likely that agriculture evolved in the Central Andes independently of areas like Mexico. In the highlands the Ayacucho Archaeological-Botanical Project has found some evidence for it in the form of a few quinoa seeds, some gourd and possibly some squash remains for the period from about 5500 to 4300 BC. During the next period, from about 4300 to 2800 BC, some domesticated plants, including cotton and a primitive type of maize, seem to have been grown and the latter was ground up with pestles and mortars. Preliminary studies of these corn cobs by the American botanist, Dr. W. C. Galinat, have shown that they were probably a prototype for the most primitive type of corn known in modern Peru and were perhaps independently domesticated in the highlands of the Andes. By the period from 2800 to 1700 BC the inhabitants of the Ayacucho region seem, in the opinion of MacNeish and his colleagues, to have been growing maize, beans, cotton, gourds, squash and lúcuma, and analysis of the human faeces suggests that coca may also have been cultivated. MacNeish does point out that his samples of the remains of these plants are poor. On the other hand he also notes that chipped stone hoes were being made and used in this period and these may indicate root-crop cultivation. Therefore the evidence from the Ayacucho area suggests that a primitive form of maize may have been domesticated in the Peruvian highlands as early as 4000 BC and that by 2800 BC it was being cultivated along with a number of other crops. As to the potato, one area where it is thought to have been domesticated at an early date is the lake Titicaca basin but recent excavations in that area have not produced evidence for this.

The earliest signs to date of agriculture on the coast of Peru have been found on the central section. In particular, in the lower Chilca Valley, on the southern part of the central coast, a refuse deposit dated by radiocarbon to approximately 3600–2500 BC yielded some plant remains. Gourds were cultivated and used as containers. The excavator, Frederic Engel, reports finding two species of beans, one wild and the other domesticated. It is likely that, when in use, the Chilca site was near a marsh even though the area is dry today. The few crops that were grown may have been cultivated in gardens situated in this marsh. At the Yacht Club site near Ancón the refuse contained domesticated gourds, cotton, chili peppers and guavas, indicating that these plants were being cultivated. At the Pampa site, also not far from Ancón, domesticated squash appears to have been grown for food.

73

Between about 2500 and 1800 BC agriculture seems to have become established in most of the valleys of the coast. The food-crop remains that have been found have not been large in quantity but have had considerable variety. For example, the inhabitants of Huaca Prieta, at the mouth of the Chicama Valley on the north coast, grew two kinds of squash, two types of beans and chili peppers. At the Culebras site, about 320 kilometres to the south, these crops were augmented by avocados and *pacae* (edible fruits) and, by about 2000 BC, by maize and guavas. Pacae, lúcuma and maize do not seem to have been grown on the central coast until pottery was introduced. Here the main food crops were chili peppers and guavas but at one site remains of sweet potatoes and *achira* (plants with edible tubers) were found, as well as what are thought to have been potatoes. Nobody is quite sure of the origin of the maize at Culebras. It appears there in fully domesticated form and was probably introduced from elsewhere, most likely from the highlands of Peru.

There is no evidence for irrigation in these coastal valleys for the period from 2500 to 1800 BC nor would it have been necessary for the small areas under cultivation. Arable land probably lay in narrow strips along the sides of rivers and overflow channels and around springs. The technique of flood farming (planting crops in areas just after river flood water has passed over them) has been suggested for some of the coastal valleys but even this method would have been restricted to narrow strips along the river bank, since the flow of water at that time, at least in normal years, is not likely to have flooded the whole of any of the valleys. Land alongside the river would have only given one crop a year, during the summer when the river was full, while that near a spring might have yielded a crop in both summer and winter.

It is likely that the soil alongside these coastal rivers was renewed annually by silt deposited from flood waters. In refuse deposits heavy duty chopping tools are rarely found suggesting that the fields did not have to be frequently cleared of vegetation in the way that is necessary, for example, in the Amazon forests. The only agricultural tools found have been digging sticks which are made of wood, have a pointed end and are usually between 30 and 60 centimetres long. Planting was probably done by poking a hole in the soil with a digging stick, dropping in the seeds and covering over the hole. The soil would not have been actually turned over with such a simple implement. It is likely that only part of the arable land was cultivated at any one time, the remainder being left fallow.

Irrigation agriculture
There are no signs of irrigation being used to grow food crops until the Early Horizon (900 to 200 BC). Certainly the coastal peoples of this period seem to have dug and used small irrigation ditches. In the upper Ica Valley, for

example, cultivated plants have been found in Early Horizon refuse at the Cerrillos site on the south side of the valley that could not have been grown without irrigation. Irrigation channels have been found on the lower part of the plain just below El Cerrillo. But none of the major ancient irrigation systems on the coast has been securely dated to the Early Horizon, the earliest date of construction for them being the beginning of the Early Intermediate Period. It is often difficult to date irrigation canals since many ancient ones are still in use and the now disused ones would have been regularly cleaned out in the past. They are generally dated by the age of the settlements to which they appear directly to relate. All that can be said at present about the coastal irrigation systems is that many major ones were in use in the Early Intermediate Period but that some of them may have been started in the Early Horizon.

By the Early Intermediate Period a complete range of crops was being grown on the coast. These included maize, squash, beans, lúcuma, achira and chili peppers. Although white potatoes do appear on modelled and painted Moche pottery they may not have been grown by these people and they certainly do not grow well in the area of modern Moche. They could well have been imported from the highlands. During this period major irrigation systems were built in each valley and these controlled most of the water of the coastal rivers. They were not all constructed at the same time. For example the system of the Ica Valley was not built until near the end of the period (about AD 500) while a large one in the upper Chancay Valley was constructed near the beginning (about 200 BC). In each valley there was usually at least one major canal from which the secondary ones led off. Recent work in the Moche Valley suggests that in Early Intermediate times the irrigation canals were designed to collect, transfer and distribute the river flood water and that there was hardly any storage. Most of the canals would have carried water in the summer, thus irrigating one crop a year. A recent analysis of food remains from a midden in the Moche Valley has shown that there was only one peak time for agricultural products during an annual cycle of food remains. This means that there was only one harvest a year.

Much of the agricultural land irrigated by these Early Intermediate people appears to have been along the edges of the valleys, sometimes in the form of terraces, rather than on the lower flood plains. One reason for this is that the land along the valley sides has light, well-drained soil which can easily be cleared of vegetation and which is still planted with seeds using a simple wooden digging stick of basically the same kind as that found on some of the Preceramic sites. Ancient canals have been found along the sides of the valleys leading to these terraces and agricultural areas. Willey has described some cultivation plots, close to the large Early Intermediate site of Gallinazo, at the edge of the lower Virú Valley flood plain. These plots consist of a series of narrow channels (about 1 metre wide) interwoven into

S-shaped or 'hairpin loop' curves. Water fed this network of channels via a diversionary one from the main canal. The excess was carried off to the sea. Near another Early Intermediate site in Virú, occupied by the Moche people, Willey found an area over 60 metres long by 30 metres wide and covered with clay-cracked cultivation plots, each about 20 metres square, once fed by a canal.

The most elaborate irrigation systems on the coast, sometimes involving canals running from one valley to the next, seem to have been built in the Late Intermediate Period. Recent work by archaeologists and geographers in the Moche Valley has traced several large canals, one of which ran from the Chicama Valley just to the north, subsidiary canals and field systems dating to the time of the Chimú Empire. The canal constructed from the Chicama Valley to the field system just north-east of Chan Chan has a length of over 32 kilometres. It was designed to supplement the flow of water from the canal system connected to the Moche river since the Chicama has a bigger flow of water. This long canal does not appear to have lasted for many years as it was built across at least one dry river bed and large parts of it on this section have been destroyed by periodic floods.

So far no concrete evidence has been found as to the ways in which the Chimú and other coastal peoples diverted water from the rivers into their canals. It is quite likely that their methods were similar to those still in use on parts of the coast. In the middle Jequetepeque a sort of weir has been built of large and small stones with a series of wooden stakes driven into the outer parts of it. On this framework branches and twigs are interwoven and the holes filled with mud. Such a structure is quite stable and, when built out into a river, effectively diverts water into the canal. These weirs may be erected as temporary structures to draw off the excess water when the river is expected to be in flood.

Most of the more important canals seem to have been relatively small, ranging in width from 2 to 7 metres and in depth from 0·75 to 2 metres. They usually had a stone lining for the sides and a stone or silt bed, although those cut through hillsides or natural ridges were occasionally cut through the natural rock. Some canals were just dug through sand or gravel and tended to leak, although such losses would have been reduced by the canal forming its own natural seal. Recently, modern canals have been lined with concrete to reduce seepage losses.

A study by an English geographer, Ian Farrington, during 1971–72 has shown that the canals in the Moche Valley were built with specific gradients so that they could water certain fields. The Chimú engineers, with a few exceptions, seem to have got their sums right and laid out the canals at gradients which were neither too steep nor too gentle. Since they had no writing how was this effected? One possibility suggested by Farrington is that models could have been made in clay, just as they were by the Inca who had models made showing the geographical features of newly conquered

To terrace hillsides to win agricultural land is a practice dating back
to ancient times in Peru. On the
coast, as in the Ica Valley today
(below), it might be because the soil
is lighter above the river bed; in the
highlands, as at Machu Picchu in
Inca times (right), it was definitely
because of the lack of much other
flat land at all. In dry regions, where
from Early Horizon times after about
900 BC irrigation quickly developed
into a fine art, terraces facilitated a
controlled flow of water down and
along the fields.

provinces. New canals could have been planned on a scale model before being built, with the distances being paced out, and levelling being done with a device based on the principle of the balance. And experience of canal building must have counted for a lot. Recently the American Peace Corps laid out a canal with the aid of all available modern techniques and surveying instruments. The local Indians who had experience but had neither the modern techniques nor the instruments said that the canal would not work. The Indians were vindicated and the canal was found to be inoperable. Probably the Chimú had much experience which had been handed down from their ancestors, the Moche.

Vegetation and alluvial silt would periodically have been removed from the canals and excavations have produced evidence for this operation. Silt was often piled up on the canal banks making them higher and stronger. During this century canal-cleaning in the area round Moche was an excuse for a party with much *chicha* (maize beer) being consumed and whole families taking part. In modern times on much of the north coast the community which benefited from water from a secondary canal was responsible for its upkeep.

On the north side of the Moche Valley a reservoir was constructed in Chimú times. It was built just north of the junction between the canal that came from the Chicama Valley and one that flowed down the north side of the Moche. It was a rectangle which measured about 138 metres long by 40 metres wide with a depth of 9 metres. The walls of the reservoir were built of stones set in a mud mortar. Water was diverted from the Chicama canal into the reservoir until it was needed for irrigating the fields round Chan Chan. The rate of outflow was probably controlled by a sluice constructed like a weir.

The fields in the Chicama and Moche Valleys during the Late Intermediate Period included those laid out with various types of irrigation furrow such as the S-shaped kind found near the Gallinazo site in Virú. In some parts of the Moche Valley terraces also had furrows. Some fields had regularly arranged heaps of stones, presumably cleared from the surface to make the field easier to work. The soil would have been cultivated by using a hoe, a digging stick or, after the Inca conquest, the *taclla*. In some areas the soil was heaped up into ridges between the furrows of water and the crops were grown on top of them. Maize in the Moche Valley is watered about once every ten days and this was probably the practice in pre-Spanish times.

Irrigation in the highlands generally consisted of trenches cut into the hillside and supported, when necessary, by a dry-stone wall. Where irrigation was combined with terracing, cut-stone channels were constructed. The Incas built some very elaborate irrigation systems and water was brought for many miles in carefully graded channels. These channels were usually built of stones carefully laid in mud mortar and they were sometimes stepped on very steep gradients, so that the water cascaded down like a small waterfall. Near and in towns single masonry blocks, laid end to end, were used, while in towns the channels were usually covered and ran underground. Terraces were built to prevent soil erosion and to extend the amount of land available for cultivation. On steep slopes the stone terraces built by the Incas were usually narrow, about 1·50 metres wide, but lower down they became wider, sometimes with an area similar to that of a small farm. Small stone stairways gave access to the different terraces and also acted as drainage channels through which surface water from the upper slopes flowed down to the lower ones.

Inca farmers

Most of our knowledge about agricultural implements and methods in the Andes in Inca times is derived from Spanish accounts related during or after the conquest of the Incas. Since there were no draught animals, farm implements were not elaborate. Of particular importance was the foot-plough or taclla which consisted of a pole about 2 metres long with a point of bronze or hard wood, a foot-rest near the point and a handle on the upper end. It was grasped with both hands, one foot was placed on the foot-rest, and the whole thing was lifted about 30 centimetres off the ground then plunged into the earth. Men used this tool to break up the ground, to dig holes for planting and to harvest potatoes. The other main tool was the hoe, which had a wide chisel-shaped bronze blade with a short wooden shaft. This implement was used by both men and women for breaking up clods, for weeding and for general cultivation. A clod-breaker, consisting of a doughnut-shaped stone set on the end of a long wooden handle, was also used to break up the ploughed earth. Guaman Poma de Ayala, a seventeenth-century Indian writer, illustrates a boat-shaped board used for scraping earth over planted seeds.

Guaman Poma de Ayala has depicted the Inca agricultural calendar in a number of drawings. In the highlands it began in August with the ploughing of the fields assigned to the government and to religious bodies. This was a great festival and chicha was provided for all the workers, both the ploughmen and their wives, who came behind with hoes to break up the clods. Once householders had fulfilled their tax obligations by cultivating these lands they tilled their own fields. The method of ploughing usually involved the ploughmen advancing in a line with their wives following behind with hoes. This method can still be found in parts of the Andes today although now the foot-plough has an iron or steel point.

Some maize was planted in August but most was sown in September. A farmer would make a hole into which his wife threw a handful of grains. Potatoes were also planted in September, at the beginning of the rainy season. As the young maize shoots began to appear they were protected from pests, birds and animals by boys with slings. If the rains were late

TRAVAXO
ƷARA TARPVMI TAV

In September the Incas planted their maize. The men made holes with a foot-plough; the women sowed the seed and covered it over.

special ceremonies were held to gain sympathy from *Ilyap'a* or the Thunder God. People dressed in mourning, wailing and holding banners went in procession through the streets. Black llamas or dogs were tied to stakes, around which chicha was sprinkled, and left to cry from hunger until the Thunder God took pity on them and the people and sent rain.

Once the rains had come in November the maize fields required irrigation and small ditches were dug to distribute the water from the canals and reservoirs over the fields. Coca was planted in December without using irrigation. Most of the rainfall came in January when the growing plants were weeded and banked up with soil. The crops had still to be protected from animals like deer and foxes and from birds. To this end the farmer went out in the daytime with a fox skin over his head, with a sling and with rattles and tassels on a staff. Early potatoes could be harvested in January but most root crops were not ready until February or March. By this time the maize was already quite high and had to be guarded day and night against both animal and, when it began to ripen in April, human thieves.

80

By May the maize was ready for harvesting.

In May the maize was finally ready for harvesting and this was carried out by both men and women. The grain was removed from the ears, kept dry and placed in storehouses; the best quality grains went for food while the poorest were used to make beer. As the grain was brought in there was a public festival with songs and dances. The main-crop potatoes were harvested in June and the early ones were planted to produce a third crop. In July all the crops were stored and the irrigation ditches cleaned.

Trade

The evidence for trade before the Inca empire is rather scanty. Also there are no signs that any form of money was used in Peru prior to the Spanish conquest.

There has been some suggestion of local trade in the Initial Period between inland farming villages and the coastal fishing settlements; the latter would have exchanged seafood for crops like maize and peanuts. The

81

A Moche mouse enjoying the maize suggests that the Incas' predecessors also had trouble with pests as their crops ripened.

occurrence of manoic and peanuts at coastal sites during this period suggests a traffic in the produce of the tropical forest. Stone bowls similar to those found in Huayurco in the Upper Amazon basin have been found at a number of coastal sites dating to the late Preceramic and Initial Periods and the American archaeologist, Donald Lathrap, suggests that trade ensued from this evident contact between the two regions.

Some of the brightly coloured feathers which made up the head-dresses of Moche warriors would no doubt have come from the plumage of birds in the forests of the Amazon. Also the coca which the Moche took would have come from the montaña on the eastern slopes of the Andes. Evidence for what may have been traded in return is not available but it may have included some manufactured items such as metalwork. We do not know for sure how the Moche kept a count on any goods received or sent. In some of their tombs leather pouches containing marked beans have been found. The soft part of the beans seem to have been inscribed with dots, parallel lines, and combinations of dots and lines. These marked beans also feature in painted scenes on some of their pottery. Rafael Larco Hoyle, who excavated large numbers of Moche tombs, maintained that these beans constituted a system of writing comparable to the heiroglyphs used by the Maya but nobody has found an effective key for deciphering them in spite of Larco's claims. They may have been used for calculations since some of the Spanish chroniclers say that calculations were made with piles of pebbles or grains in Inca times. They also tell of an abacus consisting of a tray with rows of compartments in which counters could be moved. These marked beans could well have been used as counters in some sort of abacus.

Trading vessels along the far north coast of Peru and Ecuador were mainly big balsawood rafts with a large rectangular sail. In 1526 Ruiz, Pizarro's pilot, sighted and drew alongside one of these rafts. He found that the crew consisted of men and women from the region of Tumbes, now on the Peru–Ecuador border, and the raft belonged to the city of Tumbes. Some of the men wore jewellery and were probably nobles. The cargo consisted of objects in gold and silver of considerable artistic quality which were for barter with the coastal dwellers further north. Also on board was a pair of scales to weigh the precious metals. Scale beams have been found along the coast of Peru and are frequently embellished with carvings. Those found on the north coast have holes in the centre and at both ends; the inner holes were for suspending the scale while the side ones were for carrying either two small nets or metal scale pans. Stone weights were used.

In the Inca empire trade appears to have been rather rudimentary. There was barter among the womenfolk but no money changed hands although there were a few merchants like those encountered on the raft near Tumbes. Small fairs were held so that taxpayers of each district could exchange their surplus products as well as any items which they had received from government stores and did not need. There does not seem to have been

Inca records of numbers were kept in the knots of a quipu (below left and right). Marked beans (above) were perhaps used by the Moche to assist calculations. A kind of abacus (below right) was also employed.

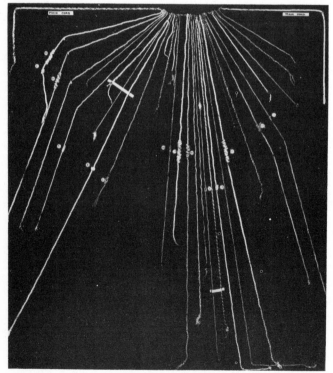

an established commercial network within the empire but exchanges took place between government storehouses, and luxury goods like gold, silver and jewels were carried as tribute from one part of the country to another. The only real trading seems to have been the housewives' local bargaining.

Roads

The tracks still used by the Indians and their beasts of burden to cross the Andes and go from one coastal valley to the next usually follow routes which have been in use for thousands of years. On the north coast between the Moche and Chicama valleys are the remains of several ancient roads, one of which probably dates to the Early Horizon while the other is contemporary with the settlement of the Moche period through which it runs. Occasionally these roads are still used. From the Chimú city of Chan Chan roads radiate both inland and along the coast. The Inca highway system, with its mountain and coastal routes as well as interconnecting roads, was probably mainly inherited from conquered peoples. However they improved what they found so that goods and armies could be quickly conveyed from one end of the empire to the other. At intervals of 2 to 3 kilometres relay stations were built alongside the road for runners (*Chasqui*) and these provided an efficient communications network.

Records

The Incas kept a tally of goods, animals and other items on the *quipu*, which consisted of a main cord from which hung smaller strings with groups of simple knots tied on to them at intervals. Many quipus have been found in graves on the central and south coast of Peru but most of them are undateable since it was not reported what was found with them. It is quite likely that some of them were in use in pre-Inca times.

Some of the quipus were used for recording numbers and their sums in a decimal system similar to our own. The knots furthest away from the main cord were units, the next were tens, then hundreds and so on. Only one quipu has been recorded with a knot in the 10,000 place. Calculations were made with piles of pebbles or grains or with the abacus described by the Spanish chroniclers.

Besides recording numbers the quipu was used as a memory aid in reciting narrative verse, genealogies and liturgical material. The Incas had a special class of quipu interpreters called *Quipucamayocs* whose job was to memorize historical, liturgical and statistical material and repeat it to those officials who wanted to refer to it. This system was a perfectly good substitute for writing and all the necessary records in the Inca empire were kept by quipu. However, it did require the special service of Quipu-camayocs.

Chapter V   The Social System

The Preceramic Period

A picture of how society was organized in the Preceramic Period may only
be obtained by interpreting the archaeological evidence. This has shown
that the earliest hunters and gatherers in both the highlands and on the coast
lived in isolated bands of not more than 100 people and run as extended
families. Such groups may have split up into nuclear families (parents,
children and grandparents) when food supplies became scarce. But when a
large mammal like a mastodon had been killed there would be enough meat
to feed a whole band and their combined labour would have been necessary
to cut up the meat before it went bad or was eaten by scavengers. Also the
actual tracking and killing of a beast that size would have required men from
several families. Although they camped in caves in the highlands, as for
example in the Ayacucho area, the mobility of the game which they hunted
necessitated a mainly migratory lifestyle. They would probably also have
needed to forage over a considerable area for plants and seeds.

In Early Preceramic times, when the lomas fauna and flora and seafood
were the staple diet, the coastal area was probably sparsely populated with
only a few small scattered settlements. In order to spread out the pressure on
the food supplies nuclear families rather than bands were probably the
gatherers and hunters on the lomas.

In the Late Preceramic Period, from about 2500 to 1800 BC, the first
signs of a more complex social organization begin to appear. Some Late
Preceramic sites, such as El Paraiso near the mouth of the river Chillón,
boasted quite large architectural structures and, although we do not know
what went on in, for example, the large masonry-walled building excavated
in the 1960s by Frederic Engel at El Paraiso, it was definitely not of domestic
size and would certainly have needed organized labour to erect it. Recently
Michael Moseley of Harvard University has estimated that the population
of these Late Preceramic villages varied from a maximum of 200 for Asia,

Elaborate vessels like this were not produced by the Nazca ▶
potters for everyday use.

86

one of the smaller ones, to a maximum of 3000 for Aspero, at the larger end of the scale. The largest of these settlements all lie south of Chimbote and it is in this area, between Lima and Chimbote, where the biggest supply of seafood is available. These population estimates suggest a need for some sort of social, and possibly political, organization. Also, in a number of them there are the remains of what appear to have been platform mounds and structures for the use of the whole community. However, the main source of food was from the sea, just as it is in modern fishing communities in Peru, and these, apart from Chimbote, usually consist of relatively independent families without a strong central authority. It is quite likely that the ancient way of life followed the same pattern. The early fishermen would have been organized to the extent of erecting public buildings and platforms but the nature of their livelihood did not require such strict regulation as irrigation agriculture. For the size of population the supply of seafood was plentiful and it is only recently that over-fishing has occurred, mainly due to the introduction of large-scale industrial fishing.

Paracas

The largest amount of information about the customs surrounding birth, the onset of puberty, marriage and death in the pre-Inca Period relates to burial customs since archaeologists have excavated quite a number of tombs. Some of the Spanish descriptions also contribute to our knowledge, especially for the period immediately preceding the Inca conquest.

Some of the more elaborate tombs and grave offerings of pre-Inca Peru are those on the Paracas peninsula, a waterless, sandy desert on the south coast about 18 kilometres south of Pisco. These extensive cemeteries, containing many mummified bodies, were first discovered in 1925 by Julio C. Tello and Samuel K. Lothrop. Tello called the newly discovered culture Paracas after the name of the place of discovery. The people whose tombs he found seemed to be obsessed by the idea of being buried beside the sea. Most of those interred no doubt came from nearby settlements such as that of Desierto recently excavated by Frederic Engel, but the surprisingly large number of burials suggests that the Paracas cemeteries may also have been used by neighbouring valleys such as Chincha, about 40 kilometres to the north, and Ica and Nazca, over 80 kilometres to the south. The earliest of the burials date to about 700 BC, classified by Tello as Paracas Cavernas, while the latter ones, which he designated Paracas Necropolis, contain textiles with the same designs as early Nazca-style pots and date to about 200 BC.

The Cavernas tombs are bottle-shaped and have been cut through the upper sand layer into a soft slate-like rock. The entrance to the tomb chamber consists of a vertical shaft with a depth of about 2 metres and width of about 1·50 metres. The chamber of the tomb proper measures between 2 and 5 metres high and 3 and 4 metres across. The floor is divided into small

◀ *Ear-rings and a pouch for coca both mark out this Moche man as someone of note.*

compartments into which the mummy bundles have been placed. These bundles are mostly about 1·10 metres high and 3·75 metres in circumference round the base. When first found the outer surface of the burial shroud is grey with the dust of ages but originally it would have been of several colours. When the burial shroud has been unwound the body is revealed in a foetal position. Offerings include gold ornaments, pottery, small balls of cotton, fragments of nets and some fish spines. The skulls have been artificially flattened, both front and back, probably for aesthetic reasons. Some mummies were only wrapped in a single shroud and were presumably the poorer people. A number of the Cavernas tombs seem to have been family vaults, containing burials of both rich and poor to judge from the quality of the burial wrappings. However, there is little archaeological evidence of sharp class distinctions.

Paracas Necropolis burials are in stone-lined subterranean vaults built among the remnants and refuse of the earlier occupation of the Cavernas people. The walls of some of these vaults are 30 to 40 centimetres thick and some have wooden roofs. In 1925 Tello excavated 429 Necropolis mummy bundles from a walled cemetery. In shape these bundles are conical and many are large, measuring 1·5 metres high by 1·5 metres in diameter. All the mummies were wrapped in cloth, made from cotton, wool or both, some of which appear to have been put on in stages. In one, four distinct stages could be determined, implying that wrapping had been done on as many different occasions. Besides plain canvas-like cloth, there are also large decorated mantles, skirts, poncho-like shirts, loin cloths and turbans, some of which are extremely well preserved. Many of these seem to have been woven specially for burial purposes since they show no signs of wear and were made to fit the mummy bundle rather than the dead person. The mummies were probably artificially prepared before wrapping by having the inner body organs removed and then naturally desiccated in the hot sands. Also before being wrapped the bodies were placed in a foetal position with the knees drawn up to the chest. Many of the skulls had been trepanned, a process involving cutting a disc of bone out of the skull of a living person. The reason for this operation in the case of the Necropolis and other ancient Peruvian peoples may have been to repair skull bones crushed by blows from a war mace. Sometimes a piece of metal was placed over the hole and the bone has grown back round it, firmly placing the metal plate in place.

Offerings placed with the Necropolis burials included small gold ornaments actually attached to the bundles. Other accompaniments included stone maces, monkeys, parrots, llama bones, meat, wool and, often on an earthenware plate, maize cotton beans and peanuts. Also found are bone and obsidian knives, implements for spinning and weaving and surgical instruments.

These Paracas Necropolis burials are unique in Peru in the outstanding quality of the textiles, particularly the over-all embroidery, and in the wide

Burial customs were elaborate at a cemetery in use between 900 and 200 BC at Paracas. Exceptionally dry conditions have preserved not only textiles, like this piece (bottom left) from one of the Cavernas tombs (above left, top), but also the reed lids (above right) of some of the later Necropolis tombs (above left, bottom). From a neighbouring valley which, unusually for an ancient Peruvian burial ground, Paracas also served, has come a pot of the same period portraying someone who might have been buried here (below right).

range of techniques used. From the point of view of burial customs these people seem to have gone to great lengths to dress their dead in the finest textiles that they could provide and must have spent a considerable amount of time making especially for the dead cloths which are in some cases about 25 metres long and 5 metres wide. As in the case of Cavernas those Necropolis mummy bundles with the largest number of the most elaborate wrappings very likely belonged to the most wealthy people but there does not seem to have been much sharp class distinction, although there was probably some sort of social hierarchy.

The Moche

The beginnings of a complex system of social organization that became evident in Late Preceramic times continued and intensified in the Early Intermediate Period. Irrigation agriculture started developing on a large scale and not only did the irrigation canals require organized labour to construct and maintain them but there had to be a strict system of water control. Meanwhile, large public structures like the Huaca del Sol and the Huaca de la Luna show signs of having been built in sections, probably by organized labour gangs. The latter could well have provided their labour as a sort of tax rather like the system that prevailed in Inca times.

The evidence, particularly as shown on modelled Moche pottery, suggests that society in Early Intermediate times was becoming stratified and also included full-time specialists. Some individuals shown on Moche pots have feline-type fangs set in their mouths and puma skin head-dresses which suggest that they could have been shamans or 'medicine men' like those of the North American Indians. Some scholars refer to them as priests but we are not sure if there was as yet a highly organized religion. These shamans were probably in quite a high position in Moche society. Other people are represented by very striking portrait heads and these could well be those of rulers. Warriors, complete with club and shield, often feature on both modelled and painted pots. One tomb in the Virú Valley contained the remains of an important Moche man who had been buried with a religious staff and a fighting mace which suggested to the excavators, Strong and Evans, that he could have been a warrior-priest. The manufacture of fine modelled and painted pottery was probably the work of special craftsmen potters just as today in Moche there is one craft potter who makes fine modelled vessels depicting the local people. The ordinary earthenware cooking and storage pots may also have been made in certain places by specialists in the same way that there are now two villages on the north coast of Peru which turn out plain earthenware *ollas* (stew-pots) and jars.

The contents of Moche tombs show that some members of society were much wealthier and probably more important than others. Some graves contain only one or two pots with a few other offerings while others have

Stripped naked, a stream of prisoners is paraded before a Moche chieftain seated atop a pyramid. The head at the bottom is a reminder that decapitation was habitual in Moche warfare.

more than fifty vessels. Presumably these disparities in grave goods reflected the differences in life between the rich and poor; the latter had few goods which could be buried with them while the former were much better endowed. We do not know exactly how Moche society was ordered but it is likely that there was a sort of pyramid arrangement with the ruler at the apex, then the warriors and shamans (priest doctors), then the craftsmen and at the base the common people.

Information about the life cycle of the Moche people, during the period from about 0 to 600 AD, is mainly derived from their modelled and painted pottery, complete examples of which are frequently found in their tombs. The tombs themselves provide our information about burial customs.

Childbirth is shown on a few Moche modelled pots. One particular example shows the actual moment of delivery of a baby. The mother is shown seated, supported by an assistant who tries to help labour with pressure on the abdomen. The obstretician is shown in front of her helping to extract the child. The apparently difficult and protracted labour shown on this vessel is due, according to the Peruvian doctor Urteaga-Ballón, to the awkward position of the foetus which is emerging with its face turned to the front instead of the back. Other pots showing childbirth depict the mother in a sitting position.

A Moche mother would carry her baby on her back in a *manta* or shawl, or held by a net in a small cradle of wood or wild cane, with its legs dangling free. Children's toys included pottery representations of animals, humans and utensils as well as rattles and whistles. Children are rarely depicted on their own in pottery and usually appear with their mothers or other adults.

Women seem to have been entirely in charge of the children and also performed normal domestic tasks. Men carried out construction work, irrigation and road-building. They worked the land and they were miners. They hunted, fished, fought wars and were also concerned with the institutions of religion and government to judge from the pottery evidence.

The dead were buried on their backs at full length with their arms extended and parallel to the body, although one or both hands were sometimes placed over the sacral region (the bottom end of the vertebral column). The head was usually oriented towards the west. During his study of the Moche occupation of the Santa Valley in 1966–7 Christopher Donnan, an American archaeologist, found some sixty-five Moche-period cemeteries which varied in size from 6 to 2000 square metres and which contained from two to more than a hundred burials. Most of these cemeteries were outside Moche living sites as is the case in the other north-coast valleys. Donnan found that the most elaborate form of graves in Santa consisted of rectangular pits lined on the sides with uncut stones or adobes and roofed with cane which was laid parallel to the main axis of the grave, being frequently bound with a simple twining of sedge cordage. The simplest Moche grave was just an unlined pit of roughly rectangular shape.

The main votive offering found in Moche tombs is pottery, usually the fine painted and modelled variety but sometimes also cooking and storage vessels. The quantity and quality of pots and other offerings varied considerably as has already been pointed out. In Santa, Donnan found that the elaborateness of the grave furniture and the complexity of the tombs themselves differed from one cemetery to another, suggesting that some cemeteries were those of more wealthy individuals than others. People of all ages, even very young babies, were usually accompanied by offerings. At the Huaca de la Cruz site in the Virú Valley Duncan Strong and Clifford Evans, two American archaeologists, found in 1946 a very young baby buried between two Moche-period pots. However, in 1970 the author found, on the Pampa Rio Seco on the north side of the Moche Valley, a baby burial without any grave offerings at all, in an exclusively Moche-period cemetery.

The most elaborate Moche tomb ever recorded was found in 1946 in the Virú Valley at the Huaca de La Cruz site by Strong and Evans. This tomb contained five people: two women, a boy, an adult man and an old man.

A Moche warrior (right) with his shield and with a club like those in the battle scene (below). Helmets were well padded to withstand blows.

The Moche people, who held sway in north Peru between about 200 BC and AD 600 fully represented the complex, stratified society that had been developing in the country for some sixteen hundred years before that. Their modelled and painted pottery provides a lively gallery of characters including the drunkard supported either side by his friends (below centre).

A well-endowed grave containing both the religious staff and the fighting mace of a Moche warrior-priest (above), and a finely wrought funerary mask with ear lobes stretched to take a nobleman's ear spools (below right). Other Moche folk were buried with less ceremony (below left) and in the same area today (bottom) it is an everyday vessel, albeit an ancient one, that has been added to a simple grave.

Skeletons playing pipes of pan suggest a Moche belief in life after death.

98

First they found an adult male wrapped in canes lying on top of a cane coffin inside which was an old man whose teeth had fallen out before death. Next to the right side of the old man, also inside the cane coffin, a small boy was buried. A woman was crammed between the outside end of the cane coffin and the end wall of the tomb. Another woman was wedged between the adobe wall and the right-hand side of the head end of the cane coffin. The crumpled condition of the women suggests that they were sacrificial victims, possibly wives or concubines of the old man. The man on top of the coffin had both his knees and ankles tightly tied together, although his hands were free, and this man too may have been sacrificed. The boy found in the coffin could also well have been a sacrificial victim. The old man has been termed the Warrior-Priest by the excavators, principally because an elaborately carved wooden war mace with a copper tip and a copper-shod digging stick with a Moche tusked deity on top were found with him. Other artifacts from this tomb included twenty-eight pots, mostly modelled and painted, a gold-plated, copper mouth mask, a copper face mask, fourteen cloth fragments and the beads from a turquoise necklace. The small amount of cloth surviving is partly a reflection of the damper climatic conditions than those prevailing at Paracas.

The Moche seem to have believed that, when the flesh decayed, life was maintained in skeletons or bones. Their pottery has painted and modelled scenes of dancing skeletons, sometimes shown playing musical instruments. In some tombs hollow canes have been found leading from the mouth of the dead to the surface of the ground, presumably with the idea of offering the deceased food and drink.

The Chimú kingdom

There is both an archaeological and a documentary record of the nature of society in the Chimú kingdom or kingdom of Chimor as it is more generally known. The documentary sources include Father Fernando Carrera's *Arte de la lengua yunga* printed in Lima in 1644 and Fr. Antonio de la Calancha's *Cronica moralizada* published in Barcelona in 1639. The Chimú had dynastic kings and when the Incas attacked them between 1462 and 1470 they were ruled by Minchançaman. The Chimú, like the Incas, maintained that before the appearance of their dynasty the area of ancient Peru had been divided into small communities ruled over by chiefs. The Chimú, for propaganda purposes, minimized those cases where hereditary rulers already existed. But at the same time other kingdoms were being formed at Chincha on the south coast and at Cuzco in the highlands. The Chimú governed through a system of hereditary local nobility.

Father Calancha's rather sketchy picture of the way of life in the kingdom of Chimor in fact refers specifically to the Pacasmayo Valley but it can also be taken to represent the general culture of the north coast.

Carrera provides a number of words from the Muchic language, spoken in the Chimú kingdom, which indicate social status. The age of the Muchic language is not known and it may have been spoken by the ancient Moche people. In Muchic *Quie quic* meant great lord and was probably one of the titles of the king of Chimor; *alaec* meant *cacique* (the Spanish word for chief in South America) and probably would have been the title for the feudal lords of these various valleys. *Ciec* meant 'lord' or 'lady' and could well have been a title of respect used to any superior. Other words indicating social status were *fixclla*, 'gentleman', *paraeng*, 'vassal' or 'subject'; and *yana*, 'domestic servant'. Yana with the accent on the last syllable is the Quechua word for servant and, according to John Rowe, may have originated from the Muchic word for domestic servant. These words for various members of Chimú society indicate that there were definitely masters and servants in Chimor. Furthermore according to the creation legend from Pacasmayo two stars gave rise to the kings and nobles and two others to the common people. This suggests a wide and unbridgeable gap between the social classes.

The Chimú king almost certainly had a court with functionaries who held special positions. A list of these has been compiled from an account of the official train of Ñam-lap, an early ruler of the valley of Lambayeque. There was *Pituzofi*, 'Blower of the Shell Trumpet'; *Ninacola*, 'Master of the Litter and Thrones'; *Ninagintue*, 'Royal Cellarer' (he was in charge of provisions); *Fonga*, 'Preparer of the Way' (he scattered shell dust where his lord was about to walk); *Occhocalo*, 'Royal Cook'; *Xam-Muchec*, 'Steward of the Face Paint'; *Ollopcopac*, 'Master of the Bath'; and *Llapchiluli*, 'Purveyor of Feather-cloth garments'. The translations of these titles are those of John Rowe. Although these people are listed as courtiers it is not clear whether they were all in fact of the same rank. The Master of the Litter and Thrones could well have been a noble in charge of the ceremonial that surrounded the litter and throne of the Chimú king while the Royal Cook may have been a commoner. Certainly at the court of Queen Elizabeth the Second of England the person in charge of state ceremonial is the Earl Marshal, always the Duke of Norfolk, while the royal cook is unlikely to be an aristocrat. Excavations in 1969–70 in the Rivero *ciudadela* or enclosure at Chan Chan by Kent Day, an American archaeologist, revealed a thin layer of powdered Spondylus shell covered with plaster on the bench along the sides of the forecourt of the burial platform. This shell-dust scatter could well be evidence of Fonga. Also in the same ciudadela Day found a kitchen area, with signs of food remains and cooking fires, where Occhocalo may have supervised the preparation of royal meals.

Although the king and his court functionaries listed above no longer exist, some elements of Chimú social structure may have persisted into the period after the Spanish conquest when Peru was a colony of Spain. In particular, local native governors known as caciques and curacas were

Moche metal-working skills were taken up and brought to a particularly high standard by the Chimú. Two handsome examples of Chimú work are a bronze ceremonial knife (right) from Chan Chan and a beaker of hammered sheet silver (left).

important in the social and economic system of the colonial period. Caciques and curacas on the coast were men or women who obtained their office through merit or inheritance from a previous encumbent. The cacique had rights to land and crops and was owed tribute in certain goods and labour service from commoners who worked the land. On the other hand, the curacas, although holding rights of their own, also seem to have administered the land of caciques. Curacas received part of the crops harvested from their own lands and their tenants received the rest. This sort of system may well have prevailed in Chimú times.

Apart from its strict divisions and hierarchical structure Chimú society seems to have granted women nearly equal rights with men. The marriage ceremony stressed the equality of both parties. When the two families had assembled on an appropriate 'lucky day' the bride and groom appeared. A new pot was filled with maize flour, and a fire, kindled with the fat of a young llama, was lit in front of the engaged couple, which they had to tend until only the ashes remained. Then the sponsor declared them married and urged them to work together and treat each other as equals. Also separate paths were provided for men and women and anyone who walked on a path of the other sex was punished.

It seems very likely that Chimú society was organized into groups on the lines of the *ayllu* (described by the Spaniards as a related group of kinsmen or a lineage descended from a common ancestor). Nowadays ayllu is used as a general Indian term to describe the basic Andean social and organizational group. In the pre-Inca period members of an ayllu were always interrelated. These Chimú clans had particular names, usually those of a place or a person, which were handed down in the male line from father to son. Although ayllus traced their origin to mythical ancestors (animals, persons or natural objects) which were worshipped, there is no evidence that the individual ancestor was identified with an animal species.

Chimú commoners could only have one wife, while the king and nobles could have more than one and sometimes a large harem. Only the head wife would live with her husband, but he still had to support his concubines, who were kept busy with weaving, plaiting and other household duties. When the head wife died she could not be replaced by one of the concubines. The husband could only look for a new wife outside his own ayllu. This was a wise precaution as it would have reduced the concubines' jealousy of each other.

The legal system of Chimor was very strict, probably in order to enforce the maintenance of the social hierarchy. Punishments were even more brutal than those of the Incas. Disrespect to shrines or civil disobedience was punished by burying the offender alive with the bones of other offenders and of unclean animals. Adulterers were thrown from cliffs (the same applied in Inca times). Stealing was regarded as very serious and the punishment of thieves was not just a civil but also a religious matter, giving us the

Public healers were at work in Moche times (above) and were later on the Chimú government pay-roll.

impression that property may have been regarded by the nobles as being owned by divine right. When a robbery was discovered a pole was set up beside the road and hung with ears of maize, both to act as a warning and to arouse the neighbourhood. Sacrifices were made to the Moon and to the constellation of *Pata* (Orion's belt) to ask for their help in finding the thief, and diviners were also consulted. When the thief was found he, his brothers and his father were turned over to the injured party for execution. A man who sheltered a thief was held to be equally guilty and received the same punishment. The dark section of the moon was explained by saying that she was in the other world punishing thieves. The high walls and narrow entrances of the ciudadelas at Chan Chan may well have been partly to discourage them.

Curers (*Oquetlupec*) were highly privileged public officials in receipt of a regular salary from the state; their curing was mainly done with herbs. If a curer lost a patient through ignorance, he was beaten and stoned to death. His body, tied with a rope to that of the dead patient, who was buried, was left above ground to be eaten by the birds. Evidence for curers is also found on some Moche modelled pots, a few of which also show a man lashed to a stake with birds pecking at him. Moche curers may have received the same punishment for default as the Chimú ones. When the Incas conquered Chimor they found that sodomy, mainly in the form of anal and oral copulation, was quite widely practised by both sexes. This custom, probably a form of contraception, seems to have started in Moche times since there are a number of modelled pots which depict it. The Incas regarded it as a loathsome vice—'a great waste of seed' according to one chronicler—and tried to stamp it out by destroying the family and property of guilty people.

We have some information about Chimú burial customs. After death there was a five-day period of mourning after which the body was washed and then buried with the knees drawn up. Archaeological evidence supports the documentary account; the burials were in seated, flexed positions, wrapped with cloth to form a bundle, on top of which was placed a stuffed false head adorned with a painted face or mask of clay, wood or metal. The Chimú believed that the dead would intercede for them.

The Chimú did not produce such elaborately modelled pots as the Moche ones depicting the moment of delivery of a baby but it is almost certain that their practices at childbirth were very similar, if not identical, to those of the Moche.

The Spaniards recorded ten stages of life in the Chimú kingdom, from childhood, through the adult span to old age. Although these were written down in Quechua, the speech of the Chimú in Inca times, they were almost certainly applicable to Chimú society before the Inca conquest. First, there was the new-born baby (*mosoc caparic*) still suckling at its mother's breast; this was followed by the toddler (*saya huamrac*) and then came the small

Feathers from the Amazon forest are sewn into a flamboyant ▶ head-dress for a Chimú leader.

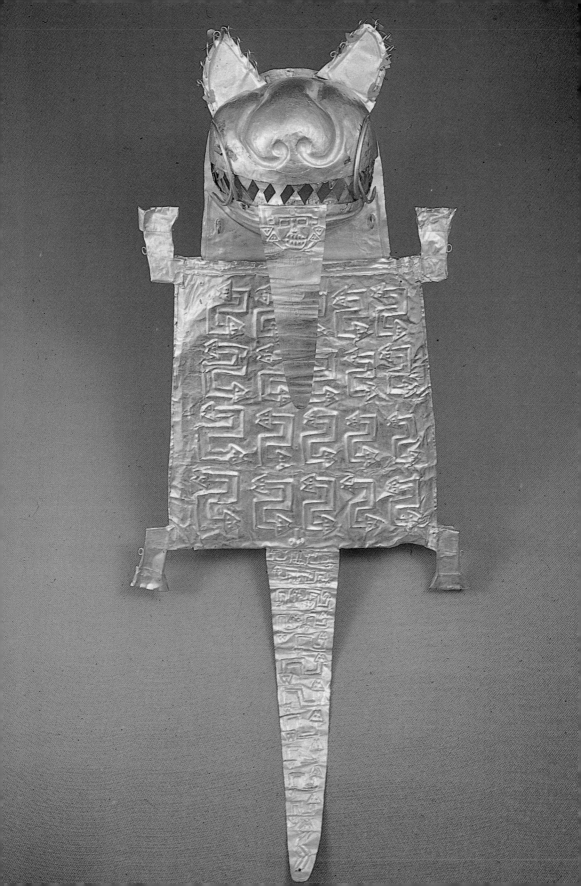

child (*macta puric*). These stages of childhood and youth continued until the twenty-fifth year when the individual was considered to be an adult. From twenty-five to fifty a man was considered a full citizen and a warrior with a right to his own home and community fields. From fifty to sixty he was regarded as 'half old', having only to do light work, while after sixty he had to pay no tribute and could not be called upon for war service.

The elders saw to it that no one should shirk his duty and this routine was adhered to under their patriarchal eye. A young man had to have his father's permission to leave home and, even when he was a full adult at twenty-five, had to get permission to marry from the head of the family. This was mainly because the couple had to be accepted into the larger household but the father rarely refused his permission. Usually a dowry or *Toma* was provided and part of it was contributed by the community. In some communities the young man could have a trial marriage but if he left the woman he forfeited the dowry and had to provide a sum of alimony. This custom was suppressed by the Spanish priests and monks.

The place and type of burial for the Chimú people seems to have depended on social status. Unfortunately the archaeological picture of Chimú burials is far from complete on account of the considerable amount of looting that has taken place since the Spanish conquest. At Chan Chan most of the dead were buried in a cemetery south of the Chimú city. These were probably the ordinary people and were probably interred with fairly simple burial rites. Once the body had been washed and buried with the knees drawn up it would have been wrapped in cloth to form a bundle on top of which a stuffed false head, adorned with a painted face or mask, was placed. Variations on this method are extended burials, rather like those of the Moche, or burials with the knees drawn up but with the body on its side instead of in the normal seated position. Ordinary Chimú graves are simply unlined shafts which may be marked by long sticks or paddles.

A number of Chimú subjects seem to have been buried in ramps and near entries within the ciudadelas (enclosures) at Chan Chan. Looters of both ramps and entries have left spoil heaps behind which include human bones. In 1970 another American archaeologist, Tom Pozorski, found a burial in situ near to the pilastered entry to a burial platform in Chan Chan. It is quite likely that these people were first sacrificed and that their bodies were then incorporated in the construction of sections of the ciudadelas and associated structures as an offering. The most important of the Chimú, probably the rulers, appear to have been buried in specially constructed platforms, one of which is usually found inside each ciudadela. The burial platform recently studied by Kent Day in the Rivero ciudadela is about 46 metres wide and 58 to 62 metres long at its base. Its central core, made of *tapia* (puddled clay), is about 8 to 9 metres high. Any reconstruction of this platform is rendered very difficult by the extensive amount of looting. Day

◀ *A priest may have worn this gold puma skin on his back as a sign of office in Moche times.*

107

A Chimú mummy bundle.

postulated, from the remains, that there would have been a central, T-shaped chamber with a row of small rectangular cells along both sides. His excavations in the piles of rubbish left by the looters of this platform produced fragments of cotton and wool textiles, Chimú-style fine blackware potsherds, human bones, and a piece of hard, crystalline, greyish-green stone which could well have been a stone idol. Most significant were over twelve Spondylus and six Conus shells both of which occur in the graves of important Chimú and have been found at other burial platforms at Chan Chan. It seems likely that this too was the burial of an important person, his body occupying the central chamber while those interred in the cells alongside were probably sacrificial victims.

At one of the smaller burial platforms at Chan Chan, Huaca las Avispas, Pozorski found evidence for the sex of those buried. Even though almost all the skeletons he found had been disturbed by looters he was able to enumerate ninety-three interments by counting the number of left tibiae (large leg bones) he found. All were young women, aged between sixteen and twenty-six, to judge from their skulls and pelvises. An American physical anthropologist, Eric Trinkaus, has found indications of birth scars on some of the pelvises, thus indicating that these bones were the bones of mothers. Pozorski was unable to find any signs of a male burial, though the amount of looting hindered a thorough search. However, it is quite likely that, if a Chimú ruler was buried here, it would have been his wives and other ladies who were sacrificed to accompany him. No doubt the funeral rites surrounding the interment of a Chimú ruler were quite elaborate and the period of mourning would have been correspondingly longer than the five-day period for the ordinary people.

Inca social organization
The Inca empire was divided into four large provinces or *suyu* (quarters) called *Antisuyu* (north-east), *Collasuyu* (south-east), *Chinchaysuyu* (north-west) and *Cuntisuyu* (south-west). Each of these quarters was divided into smaller provinces, some of which roughly corresponded to pre-Inca kingdoms. The structure within this empire was essentially one of small local groups, each having its own ancestor cult, and each integrated into larger organizational units. Social organization was stictly hierarchical with the householders—taxpayers—at the bottom and the Inca royal family at the top, with the *Sapa Inca* or Unique Inca being at the apex of the pyramid. Relationships in family and civil life were clearly defined so that all individuals, families and large groups understood their role in the province or the empire in any circumstances that arose.

The Incas extended the ayllu system from its original base of a kinship group since they found it was necessary to create new localized groups, unrelated to the kinship system, for administrative reasons. In the kin-based type of Inca ayllu, marriage was supposed to take place within the kin group and descent was through the male line. Ayllus were usually named after places or persons and not animals as is sometimes thought. The ayllus of each province were grouped by the Inca emperors into two or three sections known as saya. Theoretically this grouping was a dual one, with the two moieties or halves being called 'upper' and 'lower'.

Inca society was also divided by age groups. The Quechua language has a variety of words which correspond to our own 'baby', 'child', 'youth', 'adult' and so on which are in use today and most of which are ancient. The Incas made twelve standard age divisions for the purposes of census and tax assessment. The transition from one age grade to another did not in fact come at a certain age, since the Indians kept no exact record of their age, but rather with obvious changes in physical condition, such as puberty, and usefulness. The adult age grade was the most important and was entered at marriage and lasted as long as both parties could do a full day's work.

The Inca emperors ruled by divine right as the representatives of the Sun on earth. They claimed direct descent from the Sun through Manco Capac, the legendary founder of their dynasty. The Inca emperor of Sapa Inca had absolute power and in theory he considered all the men in his empire as his sons and all the women as his wives. To ensure effective control over such a large area both good military organization and effective government were needed as well as contented subjects.

The Inca governed through an elite class of nobles some of whom were of royal blood while others were 'Incas by privilege'. Both groups belonged to the Inca class and were allowed to wear various types of headband and the large earplugs, made of gold, wood or other material, which were worn by the Sapa Inca himself. The nobles of royal blood were members of an hereditary aristocracy descended from Inca rulers since Manco Capac. They formed lineage groups called *panaca* which consisted of all the descendants of a ruler in the male line. 'Incas by privilege' were not Incas by birth although some were related through alliances and political marriages to Inca rulers before Pachacuti Inca came to power in 1438. These 'Incas by privilege' were Quechua speaking and many of them were sent to distant parts of the empire to set an example and indoctrinate the local people with Inca culture. Those that remained at Cuzco were grouped into ayllu.

Cuzco itself was divided into two main sections, *Hanan Cuzco* and *Hurin Cuzco*, a system with pre-Inca origins. The chroniclers described this division as meaning 'upper' and 'lower' respectively. One important element in the organization of the Inca dynasty after its contact with the kingdom of Chimor was the principle of 'quinquepartition' (units of five which could easily be doubled to ten and subsequently to decimalization). Zuidema, a Dutch scholar, points out that only ten of the first twelve Inca rulers were represented in the organization of Cuzco. He considers that those in Hanan Cuzco were the primary kin of Pachacuti Inca, who reorganized Cuzco and

110

set up the basis of the Inca empire, while the earlier rulers' descendants became his subsidiary sons in Hurin Cuzco.

The conquered peoples in the Inca empire were usually ruled by a member of a leading local family, usually the chief, who was referred to as curaca by the Incas. The curaca class, whose posts were hereditary, was a sort of secondary nobility which enjoyed some of the privileges of the Incas but could never actually call itself by that name. Each curaca was in charge of the administration of local populations of 100 taxpayers or more while the Inca nobility filled the most responsible posts.

Most commoners were agriculturalists who paid their taxes in terms of work performed rather than actual goods. They worked to provide the specified amounts of tribute in food and goods that each province was responsible for supplying to the Inca emperor's government storehouses. Those who specialized in the production of luxury goods and who required tools and materials lived in the towns. They were supported by those of the Inca and curaca class who could afford them and were licensed to keep them. These specialists paid their tax by working at their trade. In addition individual taxpayers might be called upon to fulfil other obligations such as repairing bridges and they had to be prepared to serve in the mines, public work force or the army.

Laws concerning private property forbad commoners to keep luxury goods, including anything in excess of a householder's and his family's needs, unless he had a special licence from the Inca emperor to possess them. This law was intended to prevent crimes relating to property and was largely successful since it removed the motivation for stealing luxury goods.

Inca laws were recorded on the quipus for reference just like any other administrative information. There was a wide variety of laws ranging from Municipal Law which concerned tribal rights, through Agrarian Laws, dealing with the division of land, to *Mitachanacuy*, which governed the distribution of work so that each person or household did a fair share in turn. There were also Domestic Laws which stipulated that everyone, young or old, had to be given work, laid down what goods could be owned and provided inspectors to visit everyone's home to see if the level of hygiene and standard of living were high enough. The needs of the disabled and aged were provided by food and clothing from the emperor's storehouses under a Poor Law.

Laws concerning the individual were similar to ours today but punishments were generally physical and included neither fines, nor imprisonment nor most forms of slavery. Fines were impractical since taxpayers had no money and hardly any property. The type of punishment received sometimes depended on the rank of the criminal. For example, if a commoner killed his wife for some offence other than adultery he was condemned to death, but a high-ranking person who did the same would have been punished in some way short of death. Inca law put adultery on the same level as the most serious offences. If an ordinary taxpayer killed his wife for adultery he went free. However, if a commoner committed adultery with a woman of noble birth both were executed. If two people of different provinces committed adultery they were punished by torture but if they were of the same locality it was considered less serious. Women who killed their husbands were hanged by the feet until they were dead. This last item is one example of the lower legal status of women in Inca society. Even though a husband was justified in killing his wife for adultery, there seems to have been no justifiable homicide of a husband by a wife.

The use of the death penalty was strictly regulated by the central Inca government and only those officials with the rank of provincial governor and above could independently impose the death penalty. An official of lower rank who killed one of his subjects without official Inca permission was publicly punished by being beaten with a stone for his first offence and killed for the second. However, if he was out of favour he was not executed but just removed from office and exiled. Neither the ayllu nor the family of the murdered man had any right to take the law into its own hands. Anyone who killed in order to rob was imprisoned for a period of torture and then killed. The penalty for homicide in the course of a quarrel depended on who was the killer. If the dead person began the fight then the survivor was exiled to the coca plantations of the Inca in the montaña. If the killer had started the quarrel then he was executed. Punishment for wounding or causing bodily harm to another was fairly arbitrary, although if somebody was lamed, so that he could not work, then the person responsible had to support him from his own land and so suffer some punishment. If the culprit had no land then he was more severely punished and the victim was fed from the emperor's storehouses.

Among the more serious offences was the destruction of government property, such as burning down a bridge or storehouse, which was punished with death. Anyone who showed disrespect for the emperor or his government was imprisoned. Bribery was a serious offence for which an official could lose his job and, if it was a serious case, even be put to death. Sodomy was also considered a serious crime and punished very severely. Both the couple concerned and also their families were executed and their houses burnt, the idea probably being to disinfect the area. Travel was also strictly regulated so that subjects of the Inca could only move from one province to another with the permission of their curaca. A *mitima* or colonist who left his new settlement was tortured for the first offence and put to death for the second.

Inca criminal law has characteristics which reflect much of what was true of the social and political system as a whole: the emphasis laid on the sacredness of the central government, its symbols, prosperity and officials; the punitive distinction made between criminals on the basis of rank and sex; the reservation by the central government of the power to condemn to death; the placing of sexual crimes on a level with offences meriting the death penalty—all these reflected the dominance of government power, the strict social divisions and the puritanical moral streak in Inca society.

The Incas measured short periods of time like the time of day by the position of the sun in the sky. According to Poma de Ayala, the Inca week lasted ten days and three of these weeks made a month of thirty days. Sometimes an extra one or two days were added.

There was not such careful measurement of longer periods of time. A ruler was thought to have a reign with a time span of a fixed number of years. The chronicler Sarmiento claimed that the first nine Inca rulers each reigned for about 100 years. However, archaeologists and historians have dated the earliest Inca occupation of the site of Cuzco to about AD 1200 and put the ninth Inca emperor, Pachacuti, between AD 1438 and 1463. A reign of 100 years for each Inca emperor would have entailed a foundation date of about AD 500 for Cuzco which is not supported by the archaeological evidence. Time was divided on the principle of quinquepartition (five) and decimpartition (ten). In theory this system was used to divide people's lives into approximate age groups of set time and also to calculate other time spans. According to the Inca system of dividing time, five worlds of 1,000 years each had passed. A Sun had a life span of 1,000 years known as a *Capac-huatan* and every Sun consisted of a world divided by two periods of 500 years each, known as *Pachacutis*, when great changes were brought about. Montesino lists Pachacuti as the ninth Inca ruler with this name and his reign probably marked the beginning of the fifth world.

The Inca life cycle

Children were regarded as a great economic asset in the Inca empire and were probably much desired. Those who attempted and aided abortions were severely punished by execution. Once a woman became pregnant she could neither work nor walk in the fields but she could continue with her normal household tasks. Before the child was born the mother was supposed to confess and to pray to the huacas for a successful delivery. During the delivery the husband was meant to fast. Mothers of twins often acted as midwives but many women had their babies without any help, simply taking themselves and their babies to the nearest stream to wash. The mother then usually returned to her normal household work straight afterwards. Twins or a baby with some defect were considered a bad omen by the family, which would fast and perform certain rituals by way of counteraction. On the fourth day after its birth the baby was put into a *quirau* or cradle, which consisted simply of a wooden board with four feet, one of which was shorter than the others so that it could be rocked. The cushioning was provided by a folded shawl and the infant was lightly tied to it. Over the head were two crossed hoops and there was another over the feet so that a blanket could be

113

thrown over the cradle without danger of suffocating the child. A commoner would carry the cradle on her back wherever she went, supporting it with a shawl tied over her chest.

Children were, according to Garcilaso de la Vega who was brought up in the Inca tradition, strictly treated with the least possible pampering. Every morning the baby was washed in cold water and often it was exposed to the night air and the dew. Its arms were kept inside the swaddling clothes for more than three months since it was thought that if they were loosened earlier the child would grow weak in the arm. Mothers never took their babies either into their arms or on to their laps when breast feeding and did not do so at any other time. The mother would give the child her breast three times a day by leaning over the cradle. This treatment was to prevent the infants from becoming cry-babies.

The child was not named until it was weaned, usually at one or two years old. The name-giving was part of an elaborate ceremony called *Rutuchico* which means 'cutting of the hair'. Relations and sometimes friends attended this ceremony which consisted of a feast, followed by dancing and drinking, after which the child's oldest uncle cut its hair and nails, which were carefully preserved, and named it. Next the uncle and other relations gave it presents such as silver garments and wool. They also prayed to the Sun, asking that the child's life be fortunate and that it would live to inherit from its father. The name given to children at the Rutuchico only lasted until maturity.

When the Inca emperor's son was named, each noble, in order of importance, cut a lock of the prince's hair and gave him presents of fine clothes and gold and silver jewellery. He was revered as a grandson of the Sun.

During the period between name-giving and maturity children followed their parents around and learnt by copying them. Boys assisted their parents in looking after the animals and in chasing away pests from the fields. Girls helped their mothers with new babies and with the washing, cleaning, sewing and cooking.

No formal education was available for most sons of commoners since the attitude of the Inca rulers was that the lower classes should learn only the trades of their fathers and not be taught knowledge suitable for the nobility. The main reason for this seems to have been to exclude the lower classes from government.

Some commoners' daughters might be selected for education in the provincial *Acllahuasi* or House of the Virgins, which was a convent in which the Chosen Women lived—the *Mamacunas* (Consecrated Women) and *Acllas* (Virgins). In each province there was an agent, the *Apupanaca*, who was appointed by the emperor to select the girls and to be in charge of the organization of their keep in the Acllahuasi. He visited all the villages and selected, from girls aged between nine and ten years old, the prettiest and

114

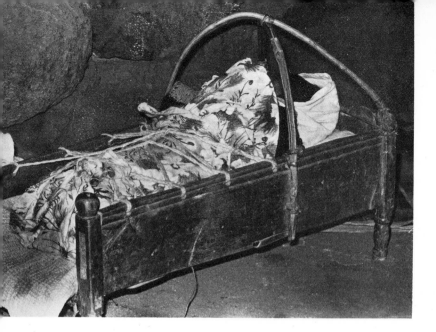

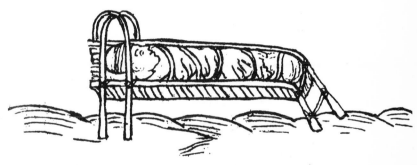

Inca children began life in a type of wooden cradle (centre) which is still in use in parts of Peru today (above). Straps hold the baby in and a cover can be thrown over hoops at one end to protect the child's head from the sun. Peruvian Indians still carry their babies on their backs wherever they go, sometimes in the cradle (right), sometimes bound in a shawl.

An Inca girl diligently spins while tending the flocks and carrying the wood home. Both wool and cotton would be woven into garments for the family and each year extra wool would be supplied with which a tribute garment was to be woven for the emperor. A pre-Inca pot (below) shows a woman spinning from a cone of cotton.

those of the best disposition. They lived in the provincial capitals under the care of the Mamacunas who were nuns dedicated to teaching. The Mamacunas taught the girls religion and how to dye, spin and weave cotton and wool to a high standard. Their training also included cooking and making fine chicha, especially that prepared for sacrificial rites. When they were thirteen or fourteen years old the girls were taken to Cuzco by the Apupanaca for the *Inti Raymi* or Festival of the Sun. In Cuzco the girls, or Acllas as they were now known, were presented to the emperor, who decided on their future. He usually selected the most beautiful girls to become his servants or concubine wives, or he could give them to those he wanted to honour or reward for their services, generally nobles. The remaining ones were kept for special sacrifices, went to serve in the shrines or to live in the convents where they taught future generations of Acllas.

The sons of the nobility and those of provincial officials had to attend the *Yachahuasi* or House of Teaching in Cuzco. The main reason for singling out the sons of provincial officials was that they could then serve as hostages for the father's co-operation with the central government and be idoctrinated with Inca methods. Garcilaso describes this Inca school as having a four-year course of which the first year was devoted to studying Quechua, the second to religion, the third to using the quipu and the fourth to Inca history. The chroniclers unfortunately do not describe the methods of teaching. Physical punishment used by the teachers consisted of beating the students with up to ten blows on the soles of their feet, not more than once a day.

The puberty of girls was celebrated in a family ceremony called *Quicochico* when they had their first menstruation. The girl prepared for this by remaining at home and fasting for three days, while her mother made her a new outfit. On the fourth day she emerged, was washed, her hair was braided and she was dressed in fine new clothes and sandals of white wool. Her relations came for a two-day feast at which she waited on them. After this everyone gave her presents and her most important uncle gave her a permanent name. A girl might be named after an abstract quality such as *Ocllo* (Pure) which was considered suitable for a woman.

At about the age of fourteen boys were given a loin cloth and a new name in a ceremony called *Huarachico* which was timed to coincide approximately with physiological puberty. The ceremony was held once a year and in Cuzco it took place at the same time as the *Capac Raymi* festival. For commoners the rites were simple but sons of nobles went through elaborate ceremonies lasting several weeks. Boys were often given names of animals such as *Poma* (Puma) or of qualities such as *Cusi* (Happy) or had titles like *Yupanqui* (Honoured).

Preparations for the Cuzco Huarachico started in October when the boys' mothers began to make costumes for them of narrow shirts of fine vicuña wool and narrow white mantles which fastened at the neck by a cord

117

Pachacuti, 9th Inca emperor and the man who led the great Inca conquests of the 15th century AD, wields mace and sling and is shown wearing the coloured braid round his head that was the main symbol of his office.

which hung from a red tassel. Meanwhile the candidates went to the shrine of Huanacauri, about 6·5 kilometres from Cuzco, to ask permission to perform the ceremony. Each brought a llama for sacrifice and the priests drew a line in its blood on every boy's face and gave him a sling. Then the boys collected straw for their relations to sit on. On returning to Cuzco the boys had to help chew maize for the large quantities of chicha being made for the coming festivities.

On the first day of December the nobles presented their sons to the Sun in the Temple of the Sun. Both the boys and their fathers were dressed in special clothes made by their womenfolk. Next they all made a pilgrimage to Huanacauri where more llamas were sacrificed. On their return the boys had their legs whipped by their parents who exhorted them to be strong and brave. Then a special dance was performed, followed by drinking and a few days' rest. Next the boys and the girls, who were to serve in the festivities, were given fresh costumes, these from the storehouses of the Sun. All then went out to the hill of Anahuarque, near Huanacauri, for a foot race. At Anahuarque the sacrifices, beating and dancing previously performed at Huanacauri were repeated. The race was from the top of the hill to the bottom, where the runners were met at the finishing post by girls of the noble class with chicha to quench their thirst. The hill, according to Rowe, was about 650 metres high and the race could have taken over an hour. Runners frequently fell and some were seriously hurt. After everyone had returned again to Cuzco, they went to the hills of Sabaraura and Yavira where more sacrifices and dances were performed. Here each boy was given a breechcloth as a sign of maturity by the Sapa Inca. This was followed by a trip to bathe in the spring of Callispuquio, just behind the fortress of Cuzco, where they took off the clothes they had worn in the ceremonies and put on other garments called *nanaclla*, coloured black and yellow. Each boy's most

118

A well-to-do Inca woman.

important uncle gave him a shield, sling and mace. His other relations also gave him presents and in addition advised him on how to conduct himself as an adult and a noble. At the end of the ceremony the candidate had his ears pierced for the large ear plugs worn by the nobility and became a warrior.

Marriages seem to have been arranged by the young couple with their parents' consent, or by the parents. In the Inca empire the couple were not considered formally engaged until they had been publicly betrothed by the provincial governor. The governor assembled the marriageable boys in one row and the girls in another. Each boy in turn chose a girl and put her behind him, but if two boys were rivals for a girl, the second one made no choice when his turn came. After investigating the dispute the governor would arbitrate and the loser would then make a second choice. When all the couples had been satisfactorily paired off, the governor ceremonially presented each girl to her future husband and gave the emperor's blessing to the marriage.

The Sapa Inca, Inca nobility and curacas had a principal wife and secondary wives but few commoners had more than one. The principal wife was the only one taken in a proper marriage ceremony with official supervision and a wedding at home. Other wives could only be obtained by way of a reward given by the emperor. Most of the Inca nobility found a principal wife from among their female relations but nobody was allowed to marry a direct ancestor or direct descendant. Only the Sapa Inca was allowed to marry his full sister; high-ranking aristocrats could marry their half-sisters but not those born of the same mother. Commoners in the provinces had to marry within their own ayllu but not within the fourth degree. In a local group a typical marriage might consist of an exchange of sisters between two men. Girls generally married between sixteen and twenty while young men did so when they were a bit older, usually by twenty-five.

In the Inca empire every able-bodied man was expected to render government service at one time or another. He might have to take up his mace (left) and go to war, man a fortress like Sacsahuaman (above) or work on the roads, maintaining the pan-Peruvian system that the Incas established and which they administered from garrisons like Tambo Colorado (below).

After the public betrothal the two families arranged a wedding following an ancient tribal custom which would vary from area to area. Among the Inca ayllus the groom and his family went to the bride's home, whose family formally presented her to him. The groom accepted her by putting a sandal on her right foot, of white wool if she were a virgin and, if not, of *ichu* grass, and then took her by the hand. Both families next went to the groom's house where the bride gave the groom a fine wool tunic, a *lautto* or man's head band and a flat metal ornament which she brought stowed under her sash, all of which he put on. Both families then lectured the couple on the duties of married life and gave them presents. The celebrations included feasting and drinking and were held in the community. In some areas the couple lived together for a while in a kind of trial marriage.

Once married a man obtained full adult status in the Inca empire. If he were a noble he might be given a post in the army or some official position in the administration. Alternatively, he could live at court or off the yield from any lands his family might own. He had the great advantage of not having to pay tribute.

When commoners married they were automatically counted in the census as taxpayers, each of whom was required by the government to perform a certain amount of work annually, which was only limited by the will of the emperor. This labour service or *mit'a* could involve working in the mines and on public works, serving in the army and in the post system on the imperial roads and waiting on the nobles. On marriage a commoner became a householder and thus entitled to a small area of community land for his family's needs. If a taxpayer performed some outstanding service he might get rewards from his superiors, such as the right to wear certain insignia, or an advance in status which might entail being put in charge of ten or fifty taxpayers.

Other demands made on householders could be for a male child of under ten years old to be sacrificed. Sacrifices like this were relatively rare and were only demanded of a father with several children. He might also have to give up one of his daughters if she were selected by the Apupanaca to become an Aclla.

At home the men were responsible for making their families' footwear. Although the Incas and curacas had servants to do this, they sometimes made their own and could also make weapons. Most of the Spanish chroniclers mention that in some of the Ecuadorian tribes the women worked in the fields while the men were in the houses, but this may have been due to the disruption brought about by the Inca civil war and the Spanish conquest and also the effect of European diseases.

Divorce of the principal wife after the government had sanctioned the marriage was theoretically impossible but secondary wives could easily be divorced. A man was held to be responsible for the well-being of his wife and if he threw out his legitimate spouse he was obliged to take her back. If he tried to get rid of her again he was publicly punished. When his wife was ill the husband was usually ordered by the priest to fast.

The wife of a commoner shared in the duties of her husband as a taxpayer by helping in the community agricultural work as well as serving him at home. She would also have had to make one woven garment a year, from wool supplied by the emperor, as a tribute payment to the government from her family. Women also carried heavy loads for their husbands where necessary.

Married women not only had to look after their houses, keeping them neat and clean, but also had to spin and weave to provide clothing for their families. Inspectors called periodically to see that houses were being kept clean, that the food was hygienically cooked and that the children were brought up properly. Women of the noble class also had to see that their household was run properly and they supervised the servants. When a woman of royal blood went out to pay a social call she would be accompanied by servants carrying yarn and distaffs so that she could do some spinning or weaving at her host's house. The host would probably give her some work that one of her daughters had been doing, more fitting to her social status than work performed by the servants. According to Garcilaso it was only the common people who spun and twisted yarn while they walked.

Quite a number of royal women led celibate lives under vows of chastity and, according to Garcilaso, they were called Ocllo (Pure). They only visited their families on special occasions or when someone was ill. These women, some of whom were widows, were much respected for their chastity and highmindedness. At the other end of the scale were the prostitutes, who lived in small huts in the fields outside villages and towns. They were called *pampairuna*, meaning 'public women who lived in the open field'. They were tolerated in Inca society as a necessary evil but any woman seen talking to them ran the risk of being shorn in public and repudiated by her husband. Brothels in modern Peru tend to be situated on land outside the towns.

Women at the Inca court seem to have had a rather restricted role in that no professions were open to married women and there was virtually no sexual freedom. Door-keepers kept close watch on the emperor's concubines to see that they remained faithful. If a concubine wife committed adultery she and her companion were put to death. Earlier Inca rulers like Topa Inca are said to have been more lenient, especially when young men of the court were involved, but later on Huayna Capac was very strict in these cases.

Once a man was classified as 'old', that is no longer able to carry out his full work load, he ceased to be a taxpayer and was supported from the emperor's storehouses. Old people were expected to occupy themselves usefully by collecting brushwood or ichu grass or catching lice which they then delivered to their group leader. In addition they helped their families by looking after and educating the children.

The Chavín 'staff' god on the gold crown of a head-dress. ▶

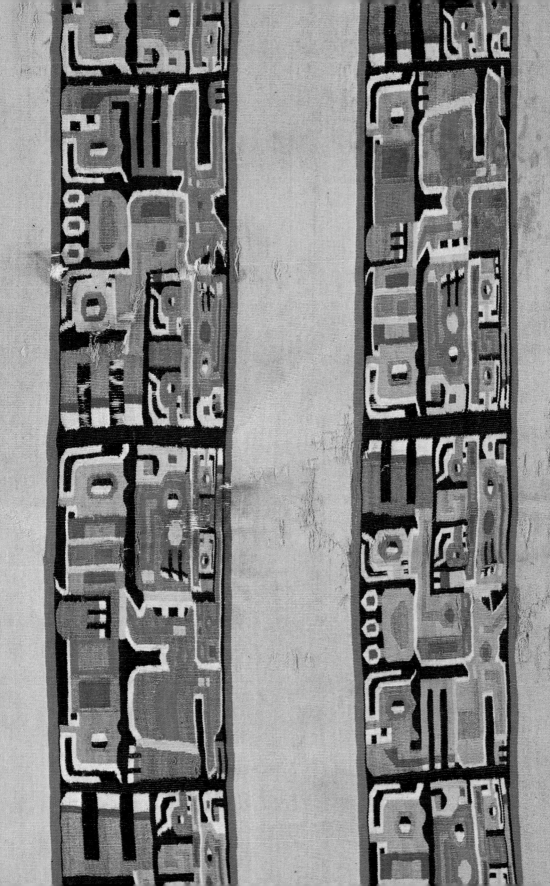

Deformed and disabled people were also given suitable work. On the coast the blind cleaned cotton of seeds and other impurities and in the highlands they removed maize from its husks. Like the old, the disabled, deformed and sick were fed from the emperor's storehouses. Their treatment was governed by special laws and regulations. Those born with physical deformities were required by law to marry people with the same type of deformation so that, for example, the blind married the blind and dwarf's married dwarfs.

The general impression one gets of Inca society is that everyone had a place in it and each received his food and other basic needs so that nobody lived by begging. Garcilaso records that in 1560, some thirty years after the Spanish conquest, he saw only one Indian woman beg and the other Indians despised her for it, spitting on the ground in front of her in contempt, so that she only begged from the Spaniards. Even today, Indians who beg prefer to do so from foreigners or white Peruvians rather than from other Indians.

Diseases in Inca society were regarded in some ways as having supernatural causes, needing religious and magical cures, but, at the same time, herbal medicines were used for their physiological properties. Although curing was an important part of Inca religion, Pachacuti, one of the more important Inca emperors, did say that he thought it was important for doctors to know about the properties of herbs.

In some parts of the Inca empire were tribes who were very knowledgeable about the curing properties of local plants, and one of these tribes, the *Collahuayna*, had to act as doctors for the Incas. A curer was called *Hampi Camayoc* or 'Medicine Specialist' and the secrets of curing were kept within the curer's family. Before the Spaniards introduced European diseases like smallpox, measles and scarlet fever, the diseases prevalent in Peru included syphilis, *verruga* and *uta*. Verruga attacks both men and animals and its symptoms are warts, fever and sometimes haemorrhages. Uta is a variety of leprosy, caused by the bite of a flea, which rots away the face, especially round the upper lip and bottom of the nose. Moche pots depict both verruga and uta.

Herbs were usually used on their own as medicines rather than in the form of compounds. *Molle* bark (from a bush-like tree native to Peru) boiled in water was used for fresh wounds; *chillca*, a leaf from a shrub, was heated in an earthenware pot and then applied to painful joints and sprains; *sasparilla*, grown round the gulf of Guayaquil, was used to relieve syphilitic sores and to kill pain.

Minor ailments were sometimes treated by purges and bleeding. People often bled themselves in a standing position by opening with a lancet of obsidian the vein nearest the place where the pain was felt. Headaches were relieved by a cut between the eyebrows on the ridge of the nose. Strong purgatives were used as treatment for worms while milder ones were taken as antidotes for 'heaviness and sluggishness'.

◀ *The divided eyes of stylized birds on a fragment of cloth from the Nazca region are also found in Tiahuanaco religious art.*

A water jar (above), painted only on the side that showed when it was carried on someone's back, and a small earthenware dish (left) would have been in everyday use in an Inca town like Machu Picchu (right).

When a baby had a fever it was washed in urine which was also used as a medicine and kept in the house. Molle twigs were used for cleaning teeth and old skin on the gums was burnt off by roasting these twigs, splitting them and then putting them against the gums. The juice from mashed *matecllu* (a herb) was poured on to eyes needing treatment and the crushed herb was put like a plaster on the eyelids with a bandage to keep it in position. To help clear the head a powder of tobacco or *sairi* was inhaled and when mixed with saltpetre it helped cure stones in the liver. Nowadays herbs and leaves are still used both by the Indians and by some doctors to cure minor ills. Coca leaves stop diarrhoea and its juices dry up ulcers. Manioc leaves boiled with salt are put on joints to help relieve rheumatic pains.

Quite a number of cures were based on superstition. For example, the umbilical cords of babies were specially preserved so that when the infant was ill it could suck the cord, thus 'sucking' the pain out of the body and expelling evil spirits and foreign bodies. Local curers, the *Camasca* or *Soncoyoc*, old people with knowledge of plants, were often called in. Their method of curing was essentially psychological and the plants they used had no direct physiological benefit.

Sacrifices were considered important for healing. The sick would first make their own sacrifices with the help of the priests, but, if these proved ineffective, the Camasca or Soncoyoc was summoned, and this person would first sacrifice to his own vision and then would try to divine the cause of the disease. If the illness was thought to be due to the neglect of religious duties a mixture of black and white maize flour was put in the hands of the sick person who was ordered to repeat certain words and blow the powder in the direction of the shrines. Then he would offer a little coca to the Sun and scatter pieces of gold and silver for Viracocha, the creator. When the illness was thought to derive from the neglect of ancestor worship food and chicha were placed either by the ancestor's tomb or in front of his possessions in a part of the house.

For broken bones and dislocations sacrifices were made at the spot where the breakage occurred as it was thought that these were caused by the anger of the place spirit. Skilled surgeons treated war wounds such as cracked skulls by trepanning, which is by cutting a hole in the skull to relieve pressure on the brain. In the Cuzco area two methods of trepanning appear to have been used, to judge from skulls found in cemeteries. One technique involved sawing two parallel sets of lines in the skull with one set crossing the other. The other method was to drill an oval of slightly overlapping round holes each of which was about half a centimetre in diameter. During these operations the patients were very likely drugged. That they survived is testified by skulls that have been found where healing has taken place after several such operations.

Payment for the services of curers, doctors, and surgeons was made in the form of clothes, food, gold and silver or llamas. In modern Peru at least

With their knees drawn up (left) the Inca dead were buried with their personal possessions and with bowls (below) for offerings that would sustain them in an after-life. Emblems (above) have been found that may also have been buried with them.

one doctor was paid in ancient pots dug up by those of his patients who were too poor to pay cash for his services.

When a person died his or her relations immediately dressed in black and remained in mourning for quite a long time—a year in the case of nobles. The women cut their hair, wore cloaks over their heads and smudged their faces with black paint. Food and drink were served by the family to everyone who attended the funeral. No fires were lit in the house until the funeral rites, which lasted for five to eight days, were over. First the mourners did a slow dance accompanied by muffled drums and dirges, then part of the property of the dead person was burned and the body was wrapped and buried along with the rest of the personal possessions of the deceased. After the funeral of an important man processions were made to places that he had frequented in life and his virtues and achievements were celebrated in songs. Some of his wives and servants might be killed and buried with him. From time to time after the burial the family would visit the tomb and make fresh offerings of food, drink and clothing.

No tombs of Inca nobles in the Cuzco region have been described, either by chroniclers or archaeologists, probably because most of them were looted several centuries ago. Quite a number of ordinary tombs have been found. One type, found in large rock shelters protected from the rain, was a small beehive tomb made of field stones laid in clay with a rough corbel-vaulted roof. Some were square, others round, free-standing or built against the cliff and they varied in size and degree of finish, some being carefully plastered with fine mud. Each tomb had a small doorway which was blocked with clay and stones at the funeral. Inside, the body was placed in a sitting position with the knees drawn up to the chest, wrapped in cloth and mats or carefully sewn into a skin. These burials were generally accompanied by food, pottery, baskets, jewellery and bone and metal tools. The dry air of the rock shelters preserves perishable material just as well as the dry sand of the coastal desert. Some tombs contained several bodies and may have been family burial places since they do not contain the rich offerings one would expect for a noble and his train.

After death the Incas believed that life would continue elsewhere but that there would not be reincarnation. Virtuous people went to live with the Sun in the upper world called '*Hanac-paca*' while sinners went to the interior of the earth where they went cold and hungry. However it was believed that the deceased still had some contact with the descendants who looked after their bodies.

Chapter VI   Religion

The earliest signs of religious practices
The most complete picture of the religion and mythology of ancient Peru is that available for the Inca period since the Spanish chroniclers took down the myths of the Incas and recorded their religious practices. For the pre-Inca period reliance has to be placed largely upon the archaeological remains, especially tombs and their contents. This yields some evidence about religious practices, such as treatment of the dead, but reveals very little about mythology. Mythology of non-literate peoples like the ancient Peruvians is usually only found in oral traditions handed down over the years. Some of the figures depicted in stone, on pottery and in textiles can be interpreted as mythical beings but names cannot be given to them nor can their actions be fully understood.

The first signs of religious rites for the dead are probably found in the child burials which Cardich discovered in the Lauricocha caves and which date from before 6000 BC. Two of the three children had been buried with offerings of food. This may have been thought necessary to sustain them on their way to the next world. Alternatively it may well have been believed, as it was in Inca times, that the souls of the dead might linger on earth and require sustenance. Offerings like these are some indication that there were religious beliefs about death but there is no evidence to suggest any formal organized religion at this date.

From about 5000 BC onwards interments of the dead in Peru were usually accompanied by distinctive grave offerings. At Chilca on the central coast mats woven from rushes or, sometimes, nets or a mantle with a wide fringe ending in knots were placed in burials dated to about 3500 BC. There is a possibility that cannibalism was being practised at this time in Chilca for under a layer of ashes eight burials were found in which the bones had been partially burned and mixed with many human and marine mammal remains. Perhaps the human bones had been roasted over a fire before being eaten. At about the same time, in burials at Rio Grande in the Nazca Valley on the south coast, bodies were clothed and accompanied by articles of daily use.

The earliest temple structure so far found in Peru is the Temple of the Crossed Hands at Kotosh near Huanaco, on the upper Huallaga river. This temple and a number of other structures at Kotosh are basically quadrangular enclosures with field-stone walls laid in clay with straightened sides and a flat outer surface. In the Temple of the Crossed Hands the walls have been sufficiently well preserved to reveal narrow vertical rectangular niches, some of which contain bone fragments, including those of llamas, or other material which could be interpreted as offerings. Between two niches a pair of arms has been modelled in clay and one crossed over the other. At the centre of each enclosure the Japanese excavators found a sort of raised frame surrounding a small patio, with a central hearth. The latter had a ventilator in the form of a subterranean tunnel extending horizontally from the base of the pit through the exterior wall. Close examination of one of these hearths showed that it was used for long periods and then restored and reused. It is not known what was the purpose of the hearths. They may have been sanctuaries dedicated to fire or could have just acted as a focus for community or family gatherings. Whatever their purpose these structures at Kotosh, dated to between about 3000 and 2000 BC, were more than just simple domestic buildings. They are the only ones of their type yet known for this period in the highlands or on the coast.

Evidence for the sacrifice of llamas on the coast has been found in a rectangular structure appropriately called the Temple of the Llamas. It is located on a small hill, the Huaca Negra, in the Virú Valley and is essentially a platform about a metre high with low walls made from rough field stones. Here in 1946 Strong and Evans found four llamas buried, three inside the temple and the fourth outside. The one found outside had both its front and hind legs tied. The skeletons of the other three llamas were haphazardly arranged, with the heads at varying depths below the surface. This suggested that they had simply been thrown into the grave after being sacrificed. The fourth beast had probably been bound before being killed. All the llamas had probably been sacrificed as offerings in some religious ceremony. The date of their burial is probably in the period 1800 to 1200 BC, to judge from the few sherds of pottery associated with them.

Chavín religion

Almost all archaeologists who have worked in Peru regard a substantial part of the art style of Chavín, especially that in stone and on pottery, as indicating the worship of a feline deity. Chavín de Huántar today is a village set at over 3,000 metres altitude on the eastern slopes of the Cordillera Blanca in north Peru. On the outskirts there is a stone-built temple. One Spanish chronicler, Antonio Vázquez de Espinosa, described it as '. . . a large

132

A reconstruction of the Temple of Chavín on the Mosna River in the Andes, showing the final spread of the north and south wings (right and left) and the position of the sunken plaza in front of them in about 600 BC. Holes at the top of the walls of the main building were the mouths of shafts ventilating a network of interior galleries, stairways and chambers.

building of huge stone blocks, very well wrought; it was a guaca, one of the most famous of the heathen sanctuaries, like Rome or Jerusalem with us; the Indians used to come and make their offerings and sacrifices, for the Devil pronounced many oracles from here, and so they repaired here from all over the kingdom'. Recently, the Peruvian archaeologist, Marino Gonzales

133

Moreno, has reported extensive ancient occupation debris from the area of modern Chavín. This suggests that the temple had its supporting settlement.

The central temple building, known as the *Castillo* (Spanish for 'castle'), is made up of four sections which seem to have been built at different periods. It is 15 metres high and consists of superimposed platforms. The oldest part is the U-shaped central section which encloses a plaza that faces east. Inside the Castillo are many galleries and chambers set at different levels connected by stairways. The interior galleries are linked by square vents which run right to the exterior, thus providing ventilation. There are also rectangular niches of various sizes which could have been used for offerings.

Originally the temple was probably covered with sculptures both inside and out but now only a very few remain in situ. Also many carvings have been found in the neighbourhood. Some of these have been interpreted as being purely religious but most were either wall ornaments or performed a functional role. Some galleries were used for offerings of objects and animals. In the recently excavated Gallery of the Offerings several hundred pots, guinea-pig, llama and fish bones as well as marine shells (brought at least 144 kilometres over a route crossing two mountain ranges) were found. The pottery was mostly in pieces but was very well made and skilfully decorated.

In the oldest part of the temple are two groups of superimposed galleries laid out in the form of a rough cross. In the centre of the lower gallery is a sculptured stone standing 4·53 metres high and shaped like a lance or a knife. This stone has been termed the *Lanzón* (Spanish for a short, thick dagger) by Peruvian archaeologists. Its surface is almost completely covered with carving depicting a very stylized figure of a feline—probably a jaguar—in human form. This figure is thought to have been an important deity in the Chavín cult. The creature has its left arm along its side while the right is raised. Claws are set at the ends of fingers and toes. The thick lips are turned up at the corners and a tusk protrudes over the lower lip. Snakes represent eyebrows and hair and a large ornament hangs from each ear. Its costume ends in a fringe but does not completely cover the legs. Both the waist and the upper part of the shaft—the 'handle' section—are ornamented with the faces of felines, all of which have the pupils of the eyes looking upwards, a typical Chavín motif. Peruvian guides like to say that human and animal sacrifices were carried out at this stone but there is no conclusive evidence for it, although one relief fragment shows a Chavín warrior carrying a human trophy head. Also the animal bones found in the Gallery of the Offerings suggest that these beasts may have been sacrificed. The deity depicted on the Lanzón is referred to as the 'Smiling God' by Rowe but, as Tello noted, the epithet 'Cruel God' might be more appropriate since the mouth is treated in a way that suggests the snarl of a wild beast. The Peruvian archaeologist Luis Lumbreras, who has recently excavated at

134

Remains of the entrance to the south wing at the Temple of Chavín (above) and one of the last to survive in situ of the sculptures that originally adorned the temple both inside and out (right).

Chavín, prefers the title 'Irritated God', though nobody knows what name the Chavín people gave to this figure. It is certainly quite awesome when one approaches it along the stone-lined gallery. The Lanzón is the only religious carving at Chavín which seems to be in its original position.

Another Chavín deity is depicted on the Raimondi Stone, a rectangular granite slab about 1·90 metres high, which was found in the ruins of Chavín in about 1840 but since 1874 it has been exhibited in Lima. The carving on this stone shows a standing feline in human form with a large rectangular head and outstretched arms, holding a sort of staff in each hand. Fingers and toes terminate in claws. The mouth has four curved projecting tusks, two from the upper and two from the lower lip. The lips are thick but turned down at the ends in contrast to the Lanzón with its turned up mouth. The eye pupils are looking upwards. Snakes represent the hair and two of them emanate from each side of the belt; the Lanzón had only one each side. Above the head-dress is a series of long complicated designs involving mouths, fangs and snakes which are probably intended to depict the god's hair. Rowe suggests that the sculptor had to fill the space on the stone with the god but the latter had to be in the same proportions as those of the human body. Therefore the sculptor filled up the remaining space on the stone with the representation of hair. Rowe has termed this god the 'Staff God' and believes that it replaced the 'Smiling God' when the new part of the temple was built. As in the case of the 'Smiling God' we do not know what name the Chavín people gave to the deity depicted on the Raimondi Stone.

At the east front of the new extension of the temple, facing the plaza, is a monumental portal, the south half of which is built of white granite while the north one is made of black limestone. Rowe has termed this the Black and

A feline in human form appears on both the Lanzón (right), in the oldest part of the Temple of Chavín, and on the Raimondi Stone (below).

White Portal. On each of the two columns which flank the doorway on this portal is a figure in low relief, with the body, legs and arms of a man, but the head, wings and claws of a bird of prey. The bird elements of this figure on the south column are those of an eagle while hawk markings appear on the north column. Both figures are standing and each holds what looks like a sword-club across the body. The position of the figures on the columns suggests that they may have been supernatural beings stationed to guard the entrance to the temple. The deity which these 'angels' guarded may well have been the 'Staff God'. Further evidence for this is provided by a gold plaque now in the Rafael Larco Herrera Museum in Lima. On it is shown a figure which has the same pose and mouth treatment as the 'Staff God' but lacks his elaborate hair. On the left and right of this derived 'Staff God' are 'angel' figures which combine bird and human attributes just like those on the columns at Chavín. Their position suggests, as at Chavín, that they may have been intended as guardians. Rowe has suggested that the 'Staff God' was probably a nature god and his association with eagles and hawks may indicate that he lived up in the sky with the birds.

There is evidence in carved stonework, modelled and painted clay, pottery, goldwork and the occasional textile that the Chavín feline figures were quite widespread in Peru from about 1000 to 300 BC. At Kuntur Wasi, near Cajamarca, traditional Chavín-type stone sculptures have been found along with three-dimensional statues of felinized human beings unlike any found at Chavín. In the Moche Valley Chavín-style clay friezes have recently been found at the Huaca de Los Reyes by Luis Watanabe and Michael Moseley. At Chongoyape in the Lambayeque Valley, also on the north coast, three large gold crowns were found, on one of which the 'Staff God' is depicted. In the Nepeña Valley there are two temples with Chavín-style elements. One, Cerro Blanco, is a solid platform of conical adobes and stones about 15 metres high, on top of which are several chambers with ornamental walls. The decoration consists of Chavín-style felines modelled in clay and painted. The other, Punkuri, is also built of conical adobes but is only about 2·4 metres high. It has a clay sculpture of a quite realistic feline with Chavín characteristics. Chavín-style felines are depicted on Cupisnique pottery, so named after a small valley just north of Chicama. They are usually shown in the form of incised designs similar to those found on the pottery at Chavín itself.

The southern limits of Chavín influence appear to have been the Ayacucho region in the central highlands and the Nazca Valley on the south coast. At Wichqana in Ayacucho Province a U-shaped ceremonial structure has been found without any Chavín-type carved stones but associated with it were skulls of decapitated women with the typical fronto-occipital (flattened front and back) skull deformation found on burials of the Chavín period. This reinforces the evidence already provided by the stone carving of the Chavín warrior carrying a trophy head that human sacrifice may have been carried out by these people, possibly as part of religious ceremonies. On the south coast there is some pottery, known as the Paracas style, on which incised felines like those found at Chavín are depicted. Also there is a textile from Callango in the Ica Valley which shows a figure very similar to the Staff God on the Raimondi Stone in that he is feline in form, holds a staff in each hand and has a complex ornamentation of snakes, claws and tusks. Some archaeologists have suggested that missionaries travelled between Chavín and Paracas and Ica.

In spite of all this archaeological evidence for a feline cult at Chavín and elsewhere in Peru virtually nothing is known of how this religion actually operated and what were its fundamental beliefs. There are suggestions of human sacrifice and also evidence of offerings at Chavín itself. The nature of the cult may be glimpsed in an account by Mishkin of the religion of the Quechua Indians in the late 1930s in the village of Kauri in the department of Cuzco. Mishkin states that there is a widespread belief in the Peruvian Andes that the mountain peaks are inhabited by Apus and Aukis, mountain spirits and guardian divinities, and have concealed within them great palaces

Moche religion revived some of the Chavín feline cult in a fanged hero who here does battle with a two-faced crab.

The Moche fanged being is often shown on top of a pyramid or, as here, emerging from a mountain top.

and *haciendas* (estates) together with herds of livestock guarded by the servants of the spirits. The most active of the spirits is the *Ccoa*, a cat-like animal about 40 centimetres high and 60 centimetres long, grey in colour with black stripes running the length of his body. His eyes are phosphorescent and his head is slightly larger than that of an ordinary cat. He is most frequently seen with hail running out of his eyes and ears since he brings lightning and hail, destroying crops and killing with his lightning. He is the most feared of the spirits. The Kauri people say that he lives on Ausangate, one of the highest mountains in southern Peru and only a few kilometres away from the village. The Ccoa could be seen as a modern-day descendant of the Chavín feline. Also the role of the Ccoa in Kauri, namely that of a spirit of whom everyone was afraid, could well have been the same as that occupied by the Chavín feline. If one assumes that the Chavín feline is a jaguar then it was probably feared in antiquity and very likely had to be appeased with sacrifices and offerings.

Moche religion

The pantheon of Moche gods seems to have been quite large although some scholars, such as Larco Hoyle, have interpreted the evidence, mainly from painted and modelled pottery, as indicating only one or two principal ones. There seems to have been a revival of the Chavín feline cult since there are numerous figures with prominent fangs and some have ear ornaments in the form of snake heads. In addition there are many pots showing animals with human attributes. These include foxes, richly dressed and armed as warriors, crabs, fish, owls and birds. Also there are maize and bean plants in human form. Sometimes a fanged being is shown emerging from the top of a maize cob. A number of these representations, such as the fox warriors, may simply be humans dressed up in animal skins since this practice was recorded amongst some of the Indians of Peru at the time of the Spanish conquest. Also modern Andean Indians have been known to dress up in condor feathers. Today in the area round lake Titicaca 'Devil' masks in Corpus Christi processions incorporate feline (probably jaguar) fangs. Possibly some of the Moche pots showing humans with fangs were depictions of a person wearing a mask rather than of an actual god. However, the mask may well have represented a deity and his spirit may have entered into the wearer. This fanged personage found on Moche pottery has been termed *Ai-apaec*, a name which seems to have been used in Chimú times, but nobody knows if this really was the name given to him by the Moche. Generally, snakes form part of his belt and he may be shown fighting a monster, often part human and part animal, which he usually defeats.

Human sacrifices seem to have formed a part of Moche religion. Pottery shows prisoners, usually stripped naked, being sacrificed to fanged beings who are usually either up in the mountains or on the top of pyramids.

141

The victim's throat was cut and his blood or body offered up to the appropriate god. The moon appears on a number of vessels and may well have been the important deity she was later on in Chimú times.

Although we know nothing about the Moche concept of the after-life there are depictions on some pots of skeletons playing musical instruments, such as drums and pan pipes, and dancing. Occasionally they are even shown making love. This evidence suggests a belief in life after death. In addition food was placed in tombs and some hollow canes have been found leading from the mouth of the dead to the ground surface, presumably so that the deceased could be offered food and drink. If skeletons were to lead an active life they would require feeding even if it were only through a tube.

Nazca religion

Like their contemporaries the Moche, the Nazca people placed offerings of food and pottery with the dead. Presumably the idea was to ensure that souls were fed in the after-life. But there are no pots showing skeletons leading an active life.

On Nazca pots there are numerous depictions, painted in polychrome, of a feline with human attributes but without projecting canines, although whiskers are commonly represented. He seems to have a mixture of ocelot and otter characteristics, particularly since the whiskers are shown projecting upwards like those of the otter. Alan Sawyer, an American archaeologist, suggests that this feline, sometimes shown with a *pepino* (variety of cucumber) in his paw, may have been a guardian spirit of agriculture. Sometimes he is shown with a bird tail and holds a human trophy head in claw-like hands. In fact there are quite a number of trophy heads shown on these pots which suggests that decapitation was practised, perhaps as a sacrifice to the feline. One Nazca burial, at Chaviña at the mouth of the Acari River, did contain the decapitated body of a man whose head had been replaced by a gourd.

The Nazca people made large complexes of designs on the Pampa Ingenio in the Nazca Valley and these may represent a sort of calendar related to agriculture. They cover an area of desert about 500 kilometres square and were produced by the removal of patinated surface stones to reveal the underlying yellowish layer. Triangular and trapezoidal paths are associated with straight lines several kilometres long and there are also huge geometric designs, animals and plants. One bird is 120 metres long while a monkey measures some 95 metres. Although the figures are clearly visible from the air they are difficult to recognize from the ground on account of their large size and because the lines tend to merge into a maze of paths.

The date of these designs has been put at about AD 400–600, which is supported by a radiocarbon date of AD 550 obtained from a wooden post found in one of these paths. Paul Kosok and Maria Reiche (both

Serpent-headed whiskers on a Nazca ornament (below) have some of the snake and feline elements of Chavín religion. But the calendar was a special preoccupation of the Nazca people and their priests may have laid out lines in the desert that sometimes (left) align with the winter solstice sunset or, like the 95-metre wide monkey (above), represent a constellation.

143

archaeologists, the former American and the latter German) have suggested that each line was equated with the movement of the stars, while they interpreted the animals as representing stellar constellations. The monkey figure symbolizes the Big Dipper whose movements would have been used by astrologers to predict the availability of water for irrigation. The constellations do not always appear at the same time each day and there is a day in every year, or period of years, when they reappear or disappear during daylight, but the point on the horizon where this takes place is fixed. These periodic motions can serve as markers and indicators of changes in the weather. Today Andean farmers can read in the stars the time to plant and to harvest.

On the south Peruvian coast it is vitally important to know when the flood waters are coming so that preparations can be made to irrigate the land. It is quite likely that the Nazca people had specialists, possibly priests, who predicted such events and devoted themselves to the 'calendar'.

Tiahuanaco

On the eastern side of lake Titicaca are the ruins of Tiahuanaco, at an altitude of about 4,000 metres on the Bolivian altiplano in the province of Collao. Of the six architectural complexes there the largest and most important is the great enclosure of Kalasasaya. Most of the buildings that have been studied appear to have served a ceremonial purpose rather than a domestic one. Although some people probably lived at Tiahuanaco and the surrounding region supports quite a large scattered population today, no ancient domestic buildings have been found. Excavations carried out by the Bolivian archaeologist, Ponce Sanguines, have shown that most of the temples were built between about AD 200 and 500.

Between about AD 500 and 800 a number of anthropomorphic stone sculptures of human figures were erected. One is a reddish pillar, 7·3 metres high, with a rectangular cross-section. In addition to the human figure carved on it, the surface is covered with incised designs made up of felines with human features, birds, human-like beings, fish and geometric frets. The principal stone carving erected during this period is the so-called 'Gateway of the Sun', a monolithic stone gateway about 3 metres high, which was erected at the north-west corner of the Kalasasaya. On the lintel is a carved frieze in the centre of which is a person with a radiating head-dress that includes six puma heads on long necks. A staff is held in a vertical position in each hand. At the lower end of the staves are eagle heads; the one in the right hand is probably a spear-thrower and has an eagle head at the upper end to represent the hook; that in the left hand divides in two and ends in two eagle heads. The latter may be intended to represent a quiver with two darts. The face has round staring eyes from which fall bands containing circles, suggesting tears. On the body of the figure, condor and puma heads are

In one of six great architectural complexes lying in ruins at Tiahuanaco east of lake Titicaca stands a 3-metre high stone gateway of about AD 600. A frieze on the lintel is dominated by a figure with a radiating head-dress of puma heads (above). This has been taken to be the Peruvian creator god, Viracocha, but is sometimes known for its 'tears' as the Weeping God of Tiahuanaco.

depicted and a row of stylized faces, possibly human trophy heads, hangs from the belt. This figure has been said to represent the creator god of Peruvian mythology, Viracocha, and at least one Spanish chronicler, Cieza de León, has recorded legends which suggest this. On each side of the figure are three rows of attendants, who run in towards him. Their faces are either like his or are those of eagles and all are dressed in winged cloaks with condor-head appendages. A locally modified version of the central figure has been found painted on special pottery urns excavated in 1942 near Conchopata, a suburb of Ayacucho, and at Pacheco in the upper Nazca Valley. The Conchopata urns had been deliberately smashed in antiquity with a blow to the face of the figure. They too carry representations of attendants. This evidence suggests that the Tiahuanaco central figure had some influence in both central and south Peru and was in fact adopted by the Huari people, whose capital was about 25 kilometres north of Ayacucho. We do not know exactly what was involved in the worship of this figure but the following legend recounted by Cieza de León gives us some clue to his origin.

Cieza de León recorded myths told to him by Indians living round lake Titicaca who in turn had heard them from previous generations and so on into antiquity. One of these states that, before the Inca conquest of that area in the fifteenth century, the Indians did not see the sun for a long time and suffered much hardship as a result. After they had prayed to their gods, begging for sunlight, a brilliant sun rose from one of the islands in lake Titicaca which made them rejoice. Whereupon a big authoritative figure in the form of a white man appeared from the south. He had tremendous power, altering the shape of the landscape and making streams flow from the living rock. When they saw his power the Indians called him 'Maker of all things created and Prince of all things, Father of the sun'. In addition he gave life to men and animals. The story continues that he travelled along the route through the highlands to the north, working miracles as he went. His teachings seem to have been very similar to those of Jesus Christ, namely to love one another and show charity to all. In most places he was called Ticci Viracocha but in Collao Province he was referred to as Tuapaca. Cieza de León relates how temples were built to him and statues in his likeness were set up. Also he was told that the large Tiahuanaco statues dated from this time. Perhaps the central figure on the 'Gateway of the Sun' is a representation of Tuapaca, or Ticci Viracocha as he is more usually known. The rays around the head of the figure could be interpreted as the rays from the brilliant sun that rose from one of the islands in lake Titicaca.

The creation myths recorded from the Collao have some characteristics of their own but also have much in common with those from other parts of the central Andes. Often they have the same roots as Inca legends about Inca ancestry and it appears that the Incas took them over, probably to explain and justify their supremacy.

Most of the myths relate how in antiquity the earth was covered with darkness and there was no sun. For a crime unstated the people living then were destroyed by the creator or were drowned in a flood. After the flood he appeared in human form from lake Titicaca and created the sun, moon and stars. After that he renewed the human population of the earth by first making stone prototypes of the different peoples, paying great attention to details of deportment and costume. In the central Andes the natives of each district can be distinguished by small differences of costume, particularly the form of hat worn. Importance is attached to a person's costume as an indicator of his or her place of origin. This practice probably dates back to pre-Inca times and myths describing human origins lay great emphasis on it.

The creator then brought forth from rocks, rivers, caves and trees throughout the length and breadth of the highlands tribes of living people corresponding to these prototypes. He gave them names and instructions in civilized life. Some myths say that he acted alone while others say he worked in conjunction with subordinate divine beings who carried out his instructions. The method of creation in this and other myths suggests that the Indians ascribed spiritual powers to natural features, such as rocks and caves, to which they attributed their origin as a group. Thus natural features or objects could be huacas or sacred places and were worshipped as a source of origin and as being responsible for the people's continued safekeeping.

The present-day Aymara Indians of the Bolivian highlands worship natural objects and call them *Achachilas*. Most important among these are the high Andean peaks, such as Illimani, Illampu and Huaynu Potosi. The Aymara still perform acts of worship to them, claim their tribe is descended from them and tell traditional myths about them. When travelling by lorry from lake Titicaca to La Paz Aymara Indians can be seen removing their woollen caps and taking up an attitude of prayer when they come within sight of these mountain peaks.

Huari religion

The principal deity of the Huari religion, which became established between about AD 550 and 700, appears to have been a locally modified version of the central figure from the 'Gateway of the Sun' at Tiahuanaco. In addition there were other supernatural beings of which the feline, eagle and serpent were the most important. The divinities were represented in an idealized form and only occasionally portrayed realistically. Human deities appeared with feline elements like triangular canines, eagle attributes and weeping eyes. Dorothy Menzel, an American archaeologist who has carried out an extensive study of the Huari pottery style, suggests that the Tiahuanaco religion was brought to Conchopata and Huari either by missionaries from Tiahuanaco or by men from the Conchopata/Huari area who learnt about the Tiahuanaco religion and brought it home. She sees the offering deposit

Apparently an adaptation from the Viracocha of Tiahuanaco religion, the principal Huari deity has, among other Tiahuanaco features, a staff grasped in each hand and stylized tear-like markings under his eyes.

of oversized urns at Conchopata as 'an expression of great religious devotion and elaborate ceremonial'. The religious significance lies in the representation on these urns of the central figure and some of his attendants from the 'Gateway of the Sun' at Tiahuanaco. The urns had been made with great skill and much effort had been expended in their manufacture. The clothing of the figure suggests that it is a male. The head is nearly rectangular with an elaborate head-dress consisting of ray appendages and feather tufts. The appendages terminate in the profile heads of both felines and eagles and also in round discs, in a similar way to those on the Tiahuanaco figure but not always arranged in the same way. The Conchopata figure has a staff grasped in each hand, a fanged mouth, vertically divided eyes and face markings below the eyes, all of which are Tiahuanaco features. These Conchopata urns originally measured between two-thirds to three-quarters of a metre high, with the diameter of the mouth slightly exceeding that of the height, while the walls varied in thickness from three to six centimetres. This type of pottery was unique and nothing else like it was being made then in that area. For this reason Menzel refers to it as ceremonial or offering pottery.

On the knoll of Robles Moqo at Huari fragments of outsize painted pottery vessels of similar dimensions to those encountered at Conchopata have been found. They carry polychrome depictions of the deity and other supernatural being similar to those on the Conchopata vessels but have ears of maize associated with them. The precise significance of these ears of maize is not known. No building at Huari has been securely identified as a temple.

Stone carvings found at Huari bear some similarity to those found at Tiahuanaco, as in their elaborate trapezoidal head-dress with four points, but they do not show the supernatural beings that are depicted on the Conchopata and Robles Moqo pottery. One statue shows someone holding what appears to be a trophy head in one hand, indicating that human sacrifice may have been practised at Huari.

Menzel's study of the Huari pottery style has shown that their religious motifs were gradually adopted for secular pottery and she suggests that the religion was itself becoming secularized by about AD 800 to 900.

It is hard to estimate the exact extent of Huari religious influence but it probably corresponded to the area over which Huari held political sway. At about AD 800 Lumbreras sees this as extending on the coast from Lambayeque in the north to just south of Camana in the south and in the highlands from Cajamarca in the north to Sicuani in the south. The most important provincial centre for Huari religion seems to have been at Pacheco in the upper Nazca Valley. Here outsize urns of the religious/ceremonial type are painted with polychrome representations of both male and female versions of the deity shown on the Conchopata urns. The distinction between male and female has been made by Menzel on the basis of their dress. The female has maize ears not only as decorations to her garment but also as ray appendages round her head and on her staff while the male only has them as ray appendages round his head. His other appendages are feline heads which the female lacks. The urns are from 64 to 66 centimetres high and 75 to 78 centimetres in diameter with flaring sides that become slightly convex in the upper part of the body, a flat sharply edged bottom and two vertical strap handles set at about midpoint of the height. The male and female deity alternate in four vertical panels on the outside and four on the inside of the vessel. The four figures on the inside are full length and fill the height of the urn.

This male and female concept is present today in Indian myths about two mountain peaks which face each other. Outside Potosi in Bolivia the mountains of San Juan de Parichata and Tata Turqui are worshipped as the male and female Achachilas of the region. This belief in male and female objects of worship is probably a survival from antiquity but not necessarily from the time when the Pacheco urns were made (between AD 600 and 700).

The influence of Huari religion also seems to have been quite strong at Pachacámac. Recently, an elongated wooden post carved with figures possessing attributes of Huari divinities has been found. The upper part shows a man holding a bola (a round stone ball attached to two others by strips of leather thonging and used for hunting) and wearing a large chest ornament. On the other parts of the post are shown two-headed snakes, felines and a figure similar to the 'angels' on the 'Gateway of the Sun' at Tiahuanaco. Also Uhle found numerous examples of Huari-style pottery at Pachacámac, which he termed 'Coastal Tiahuanaco'. Recent studies of the history and distribution of Quechua have suggested that Pachacámac was one of the centres of dispersal for that language during the period of Huari influence. Possibly the oracle of Pachacámac encountered by the Spaniards became established at this time. Certainly the earliest pottery found by Uhle round the ruins of the temple that probably housed the oracle dates to about AD 600, a time when Huari was beginning to extend its influence to the south and central coast. Later, as the influence of Huari began to decline after AD 900, Pachacámac seems to have emerged as a religious centre in its own right, complete with its well known oracle.

Chimú religion

There are several documentary accounts of Chimú religion, of which the most important are probably those of Father Fernando de la Carrera and Fr. Antonio de la Calancha, both of the seventeenth century.

Calancha makes no mention of a Chimú creator-god but this does not mean that they did not believe in one. Carrera makes a literal translation of 'creator' and uses the Yunca word *aiapaec* from the verb 'to make' as the title of God in his catechism. Larco Hoyle assumed this to be the name of the creator-god of the Moche while other archaeologists have suggested that he

A fanged being appears on a Chimú pot but was perhaps an archaic concept by then for the Sun, the Moon, the Stars and the Sea were the chief Chimú deities.

was the creator-god of the Chimú. We do not really know if the Chimú believed in a creator-god, nor, if so, what he was called.

In the Pacasmayo area, part of the Chimú empire, the Moon, called *Si*, was the greatest divinity. She was believed to be more powerful than the sun because she appeared by day and by night. Eclipses of the moon were occasions for rejoicing since they marked victories of the moon over the sun but eclipses of the sun were marked by mourning and sorrowful dances were performed. The state of the weather and the growth of the crops were both attributed to the moon. In the valley of Pacasmayo there was a great temple of the moon called *Si-an* (House of the Moon) where sacrifices were made to her. These included children who at about five years old were slaughtered on piles of cotton cloth with offerings of fruit and chicha in the belief that they would thus be deified. Other sacrifices to the Moon included animals and birds. Archaeologists have not been able securely to identify this temple of the moon but it may have been in the now ruined city of Pacatnamú on the north bank of the Jequetepeque Valley.

Although the Sun was thought to be an inferior supernatural being he was believed to be the father of holy stones called *alaec-pong* or cacique stones. These appear to have stood out in the open and were just natural boulders. They were said to be sons of the Sun and ancestors of the people in whose district they stood. The Sun had turned them to stone in anger because of the death of their mother. Rowe points out that these alaec-pong corresponded very closely to the *wanka* or field-guardians of Inca religion.

There were several important constellations of which the most notable was probably *Fur* (the Pleiades). Fur was the patron of agriculture and watched over the crops. Each appearance of this constellation marked the beginning of a new year. Neither the sun nor the moon features in the calendar. Another important constellation was *Pata* (Orion's Belt). This consists of a row of three stars and the Chimú believed that the middle one was a thief while those on either side were emissaries of the Moon sent to feed him to the vultures, which were represented by four stars immediately below. The Morning and Evening Stars (two aspects of Venus) were called *Ni* (also the word for the sea) but we do not know whether Venus was worshipped.

The Chimú empire was a coastal one and therefore it is not surprising to find that the sea was worshipped. The Sea or *Ni* was an important divinity to whom sacrifices of white maize flour, red ochre and other things were made together with prayers for fish and protection against drowning. Only the whale was regarded as sacred, probably on account of its size. All other sea creatures were regarded merely as food.

As was the custom in other parts of Peru, each district had its local shrines or huacas, each of which had its own sacred object of worship (*mac aec*), legend and cult. Some were important, such as the temple of Chot, while others were just homes of popular witches like one called Mollep (The

Lousy). Calancha recounts how Mollep lived at Coslechec in Talambo (Pacasmayo) and was very dirty, telling the people that just as his lice multiplied so would they. Rowe has suggested that the temple of Chot was what is now known as the Huaca Chotuna, located on the south side of the Chicama Valley. In the course of trying to stamp out idolatry in the seventeenth century Roman Catholic priests left descriptions of some of the huacas. One, called Corquin, contained the following cult objects: a long scabby-looking stone to which sacrifice was made for protection against leprosy, mange and smallpox; a small green stone idol representing an ancestor; and three small green stones believed to be ancestors of chili pepper, beans and wheat. The wheat ancestor would have been invented after the Spanish conquest since it was unknown in Peru before that.

Fasting in the Chimú empire consisted of abstaining from chili pepper, salt and sexual intercourse. When there was a famine, not only did the people fast but they made their domestic animals—dogs, guinea pigs and ducks—fast as well.

Some of the gods had symbolic animals such as the fox which, being both diurnal and nocturnal, was symbolic of Si, the Moon. The appearances of certain birds, such as the owl, were interpreted as omens. The gods also gave advice through oracles in huacas. There seem to have been quite a number of witches, both male and female. Calancha relates a description he obtained from Luis de Teruel of a meeting of a kind of witches' guild at Huamán, about 3 kilometres south of Trujillo, which involved ceremonial cannibalism and ended with a sexual orgy. One witch went into a trance and claimed he had been to a place about 3·5 kilometres away while he was unconscious. Another was believed to be able to turn himself into a dog or an owl.

Today the witches on the north coast and elsewhere in Peru are called *brujos* and can be classified as good and bad, depending on what they practise. The good ones act as curer, with the aid of herbs and magical apparatus. And there is one in Moche who claims to be able to communicate with other people far away by a sort of telepathy. These modern brujos are probably the descendants of the witches who practised in Chimú times.

Inca beliefs
When the Incas conquered an area they allowed its inhabitants to continue worshipping their old idols and sacred places provided that they also complied with demands made on them by the Inca religious authority. Where the Incas found ancient and well-known oracles and shrines, such as that at Pachacámac, they showed them respect.

Inca religion was mainly concerned with organization, especially that of the food supply, and ritual rather than mysticism and spirituality. Divination was regarded as an important prerequisite to any action. Nearly every religious rite was accompanied by sacrifices. It was particularly important for the individual to ensure that the supernatural forces of the environment were kept in a benevolent mood, otherwise physical and economic misfortune might befall him. This was particularly important in the mountains where landslides were frequent and earthquakes occurred quite regularly.

The supreme god was the Creator of the Sun, Moon and other supernatural beings, and of animals and men and ruled rather like the Inca emperor ruled his empire. The Spaniards saw several statues of him represented as a man in various temples. The most important one in Cuzco showed him as a standing figure of solid gold, about the size of a 10-year-old boy, with his right arm raised as if in command and the right hand clenched except for the thumb and forefinger. The Creator is usually called Viracocha by the Spanish chroniclers although he originally appears to have had a series of titles of which the most usual has been translated by Rowe as 'Ancient foundation, lord, instructor of the world' (from the Quechua *Ilya-Tiqsi Wiraqoca Pacayacaciq*).

It is not always easy to assess the nature of Viracocha. He can be seen as the theoretical source of all divine power but the actual administration of his creation was left to assistant supernatural beings like the Sun. Viracocha lived in the heavens and appeared to men during crises.

The myths about Viracocha's creation and subsequent journey are very similar to those recorded by Cieza de León from near lake Titicaca. Viracocha first created a world of earth and sky but left it in darkness. Then he went on to create the Sun, Moon, Thunderbolt, Stars, Earth and Sea and finally men, who were created in his own likeness. The latter are said to have been carved in stone in the shape of giants who, after a while, displeased him so that he destroyed them by turning them to stone at Tiahuanaco, Pucara and other places. The rest were drowned in a great flood from which he saved only two assistants.

Next he created a new race of his own size to replace the giants he had destroyed. He gave light to the world by making the Sun and Moon emerge from the Island of Titicaca. The Moon was originally brighter than the Sun but the latter grew jealous and threw ashes in the Moon's face, thus making her darker. Viracocha then went to Tiahuanaco where he made clay models of animals by species and men by tribe. After painting the clothes that they were to wear on the models of the men he gave them their customs, food, languages and songs. He then ordered them to descend into the earth and emerge from caves, lakes and hills in the districts where he had told them to settle. Next he set out towards the north with two assistants to call the tribes out of the earth and see if they were obeying his commands.

Viracocha seems to have travelled along the line of the Inca mountain road while one assistant went along the coast and the other inspected the edge of the eastern forests. Viracocha was not recognized by many people

At Machu Picchu (above), at Cuzco and at Pisac are great stones of unique design called Intihuatana which in the Quechua language of the Incas means 'sun stone'.

since his appearance was just that of an old man with a staff. At Cacha (now called San Pedro, between lake Titicaca and Cuzco) he was stoned because the people did not like strangers. He called down a fire from heaven which began to burn the rocks on the hill around him and so frightened the people that they begged him to save them. Taking pity on them, he put the fire out with a blow from his staff. The burned hill remained to remind them of his power and mercy and in his honour the local people built a shrine. Later the Incas built a great temple there. The 'burned hill' at Cacha is in fact a mass of cinders and lava from the volcano of Tinta.

After the Cacha episode Viracocha continued to Urcos, near Cuzco, where he called on the inhabitants to emerge from a mountain. They honoured him during his visit and later built a shrine to him on the mountain. He continued to Cuzco and then journeyed to the province of Manta on the coast of Ecuador. Here he bade farewell to his people and set out across the Pacific walking on the water.

Rowe suggests that this creation myth is probably based on a number of older local legends which were put together under Inca supervision at the end of the fifteenth century. He goes on to point out that the most important events took place in Aymara territory, including the region round lake Titicaca, and they were probably derived from Aymara creation myths. This explains the similarity between the Viracocha creation myths told by the Incas and those concerning Tiahuanaco told to Cieza de León.

The most important servant of the Creator was the Sun, believed to be the divine ancestor of the Inca dynasty. The Sun's cult was very important, given the harsh climate of the high Andes, and he protected and matured crops. He was thought of as male and usually seems to have been depicted by a golden disc with rays and a human face. One of these discs, which fell into Spanish hands, was said to be the size of a man.

Both Indians and Spaniards called the large government-built sanctuaries 'sun temples' and the fields which supported the religious officials and the 'Chosen Women' are referred to as being 'of the sun'. However the 'Temple of the Sun' in Cuzco not only housed the image of the Sun but also those of all the Inca sky gods and lesser supernatural ones. The 'fields of the Sun' not only provided for the Sun cult but also supported other cults, including local ones. Although the Sun was a very important power in Inca religion he was in reality only one of the many great powers recognized in official worship.

Next in importance to the Sun was the Thunder God, the servant and messenger of the Sun, to whom prayers were addressed for rain. In the highlands his worship was associated with the representation of Venus as the Morning Star. He was pictured as a man in the sky holding a war club in one hand and a sling in the other and wearing shining garments. The crack of his sling made the thunder, the lightning was the flash of his garments as he turned and his slingstone was the lightning bolt. He drew the water for rain from the Milky Way. Blas Valera tells how the rain was kept in a jug belonging to his sister and when he broke it with a well-aimed slingstone the rain fell. The Thunder God was called *Ilyap'a* or *Illapa* (a Quechua word meaning lightning-flash).

The Moon, known as *Mama-Quilla* (Mother Moon), was a woman and wife of the Sun. The Inca emperor was the representative of the Sun on earth while his sister-wife, the Coya, was associated with the Moon. She was important in calculating the months and regulating the festival calendar. She was worshipped in a separate shrine from that of the Sun. Her shrine was ornamented with silver and served by priestesses. The Indians believed that an eclipse of the moon was caused by a puma or snake trying to devour her and they made all possible noise to scare off the attacker, threatening it with their weapons. This custom has survived to the present day in Cuzco.

The Stars, with Venus being the chief representative, were seen as children of the Sun and the Moon. They and the constellations were believed to be patrons of certain human activities. The Pleiades (*Collca* in Quechua, meaning granary) were believed to watch over the preservation of seed and marked certain agricultural seasons. Another group of stars, the Lira or Cross (*Urcuchillay* meaning a vari-coloured llama) watched over the flocks. In addition there were stars that watched over wild animals such as *Machaqway* ('little snake') the patron of snakes.

Pacha-mama (Mother Earth) was a female deity associated with agriculture and ranked with the sky gods. She was represented by a long stone which was placed in the fields, worshipped and asked to protect and fertilize the fields. The Coya was the patroness of agriculture and closely connected with Pacha-mama. Murua recounts how Huayna Capac, the father of Atahualpa, set up his mother's mummy as an oracle for Pacha-mama in Tomebamba.

The mother of lakes and water in the highlands and the mother of the sea was known as *Mama-cocha*. She was mainly worshipped by the coastal fishermen.

All the other supernatural powers worshipped by the Incas were associated with either places or objects and were usually referred to as huacas. The Indians, according to Rowe, appear to have believed that the object was the supernatural being and that the two did not have a separate existence.

Huacas were very numerous as shown by Cobo's chronicle which lists over 350 in a radius of 33 kilometres or so round Cuzco. He describes them as being conceived in groups on imaginary lines each of which radiated from the centre of Cuzco. Each of these lines was called a *ceque*. In Cuzco the maintenance of the huacas lying on these ceque lines was assigned to particular social groups into which the population of the town was divided. A system of huacas following the Cuzco plan was set up by Huayna Capac at Tomebamba (now in southern Ecuador). Similar ceque systems may have radiated from other highland towns but there does not seem to be any evidence for them on the coast.

Huacas found round Cuzco included temples, tombs of ancestors, stones, fountains, springs, calendar markers, hills, bridges, houses, palaces, prisons and quarries. Places referred to in Inca mythology or associated with past Inca emperors were also huacas. Some of the most important huacas were worshipped as the residences of important natural powers. A flat place in one of the squares in Cuzco was supposed to be the home of the Earthquake while the Wind lived in a doorway in one of the palaces. The places where the traveller caught his first and last glimpses of Cuzco were important shrines, suggesting that the city itself was sacred.

The most important huaca was Huanacauri which the chroniclers described as a 'spindle-shaped unwrought stone' situated on Huanacauri hill near Cuzco. According to one myth, the stone represented Ayar Uchu, one of the brothers of Manco Capac, the legendary founder of the Inca dynasty, and the special patron of religion for the Inca family and youths. Huanacauri was particularly important in maturity rites. The supernatural power of a hill or mountain usually varied in direct proportion to its height and all snow-capped peaks were important deities. The peaks of Ausangate (visible from Cuzco), Vilcanota and Coropuna were revered by many. Mountain-worship is an important element in modern Quechua religion and mountain peaks are called *Apo* meaning 'Lord', but this title does not seem to have been used in the ancient religion.

In cultivated fields there are two kinds of huacas: the boundary markers or *Saywa* and the field guardians or *Wanka*. Field guardians were long stones set up in the centre of the field. The most important Wanka of Cuzco was believed to be a brother of Manco Capac.

A special type of huaca was the *apacita*, a pile of stones marking the top of a pass or any other critical point on a road, where travellers stopped to make small offerings and prayed for strength before continuing. The offerings generally consisted of things of little value such as worn-out sandals or another stone added to the pile. This custom is still observed in the Andes along roads and paths where the Indians travel on foot, and the ancient huacas are constantly being added to.

Inca religious practices

Inca temples were not intended to shelter congregations but rather to house the cult objects (objects connected with religious beliefs), to accommodate priests and attendants and to provide storage space for regalia. The most sacred Inca temple, 'The Temple of the Sun' in Cuzco, was built with at least six one-room buildings grouped round an open courtyard and surrounded by a blank enclosure wall. The Spaniards described this building as being lavishly decorated with gold plating which was siezed as part of Atahualpa's

To the Incas many natural features had supernatural powers and were to be worshipped. At
certain points along a road, for example, it was
and still is Peruvian Indian practice to say a
prayer and add another stone to a pile (above).
Among other pre-Christian rituals still observed
by today's Indians is a ceremony to ensure the
fertility of the herds (right and below).

ransom and melted down. Some of the original stone walls still stand today, undamaged by earthquakes after 500 years. The temple was mainly used as living quarters for the priests and consecrated women and also for storage. Usually only the priests, consecrated women and Inca officials were allowed to enter the temples while most of the ceremonies were conducted in the open air. The majority of the great Inca ceremonies took place in the Great Square of Cuzco or in one of the smaller squares near the Temple of the Sun. The cult objects were brought out into the square and divination, sacrifice, prayer, dancing and drinking were all carried out in public.

The Inca emperor was the chief custodian of the Sun and visited the temples and their estates, and the oracles. The high priest of the temple in Cuzco was probably a close relation of the Inca and was also the head of the hierarchy of priests in the empire. Under the high priest were the *Hatun Uillca*, who seem to have been rather like bishops since each was head of one of the ten dioceses into which the country was divided. Under the Hatun Uillca came the ordinary priests or *Yana Uillca*.

There was at least one resident attendant for all the important shrines while the larger ones would have quite a large staff including diviners, sacrificers and caretakers. 'Sun Temples', shrines of the official cult, had a group of Mamacunas who were sworn to perpetual chastity and were occupied in weaving textiles used as garments by the priests, and preparing chicha for festivals, and were used as sacrifices. These women formed a sort of order over which presided a high priestess who was always of noble birth and supposed to be the Sun's wife. In Cuzco and in other Inca temples they were responsible for serving the shrine of the Moon and carrying her silver image.

The Incas prayed both silently and aloud and prayers could either be in the form of standard phrases or be made up to fit the occasion. The gesture of reverence, the *mocha*, before a deity or emperor consisted of a low bow from the waist with arms outstretched above the level of the head. The worshipper made a kissing noise with his lips, brought his hands to his lips and kissed his fingertips. At great public ceremonials the prayers were traditional and may have originally been composed by past Inca emperors or high priests. As sin was considered likely to cause the gods anger and bring bad luck, confession was thought to be necessary for worship and was made to a priest who would test the truth of it by divination. If the would-be confessor was found to be telling lies or half-truths a stone would be dropped on his back. Otherwise the priest would keep the revelations secret. The Inca emperor would confess in private, direct to the Sun, and request his intercession with the other gods.

Cleansing and fasting were essential for most festivals and ceremonies for they nearly always included worship. Fasting usually involved abstaining from meat, salt, spices and sexual relations. Fast days before feasts were carefully observed and varied from two to six days in length.

Cieza de León says that the most devout of the Indians or the person closest to the gods was asked to fast for a year for the good health of everyone. This kind of fast might start when the maize was sown and last until it was harvested. The emperor retired to fast in isolation before his coronation or before important decisions, the latter being accompanied by sacrifices to the gods and consultation of the oracles.

The Incas believed that divination was necessary before any important action was taken. In addition it was practised to diagnose disease, locate lost property and choose between possible heirs. One divination ceremony, the *Calpa* ('strength'), was performed to assess the outcome of a military campaign. A llama was sacrificed, then the priest removed a lung and blew into one of its veins, then, observing the markings on the surface of the lung, divined the outcome of the campaign. These markings were also consulted when assessing a suitable heir for the succession. For less important cases a guinea-pig or even a bird was used.

The oracle was the most direct type of divination and a few of them had such prestige that people came to consult them from all over the empire. They included *Apo-Rimaq* ('lord oracle'), whose shrine was on the banks of the Apurimac River near Cuzco, Pachacámac, and Rimac near Lima. Apo-Rimac was a building inside which was a tree trunk decorated with golden breasts and a sash and dressed in fine women's clothing, with a row of smaller figures on each side. Both the figures and their garments were stained with blood from sacrifices. Generally the oracle had to be interpreted by a priest.

There were quite a number of simple methods of divination. One involved counting a pile of small objects such as beans, maize, kernels, pebbles and pellets of llama dung, to see if they came out odd or even. The pebbles were usually thought to have a magical origin, which was either that they were received in a dream from the Thunder God or a huaca or that a woman had borne them after being made pregnant by the Thunder in the fields on a stormy day.

Local sorcerers, known as *Omo*, usually practised black magic in secret and were feared. The Incas condemned them on account of any harm they might cause. They were consulted on small problems and claimed that they spoke directly with spirits in the dark. Some noises made by animals, such as the hooting of an owl or howling of a dog, foretold a death. Certain animals, like snakes, lizards, spiders, toads and moths, were regarded as bad omens when seen about the house, possibly because sorcerers spoke with these creatures.

Many sacrifices were made as part of certain festivals. The type of sacrifice made to the different dieties and huacas varied with the occasion and the priests would often determine by divination the most acceptable offering. Many of the objects sacrificed came from the flocks and fields dedicated to religion, of which a part was assigned to each huaca.

161

Llamas or guinea-pigs, and, more rarely, birds, were the most general public sacrifices. The blood of sacrificial victims was offered to the appropriate idol and smeared over it. The most valuable sacrifice was a human being, known as *Capaccocha*. This was only offered to the most important divinities and huacas at times of crisis like defeats in war, famine or pestilence. Up to 200 children were sacrificed at the coronation of a new emperor. When a new province was conquered, a few of the most handsome inhabitants were brought to Cuzco and sacrificed to the Sun in thanks for victory. The other victims were girls and boys collected from the provinces as part of the regular taxation or offered by their parents in times of great need. They had to be physically perfect, the boys aged about ten, the girls between ten and fifteen. The girls were selected from those already in the Acllahuasi. The children were feasted before being sacrificed, the older ones being intoxicated first, so that they would go happy and well-fed to the next world. They were made to walk round the idol two or three times and then they were strangled with a cord or had their throats cut or their hearts were cut out and offered still beating to the deity. The priest usually drew a line in the victim's blood across the face of the idol or royal mummy bundle but sometimes the blood was smeared all over the idol.

Some deities had different coloured llamas sacrificed in their honour so that, for example, pure white ones were offered to the Sun and brown ones to Viracocha. Other sacrifices included maize flour, wool and llama fat. Nearly every sacrifice included an offering of fine clothing which was burned alone or wrapped round wood-carvings representing human beings. The most important vegetable offering were coca leaves, which were burnt. Small lumps of gold and silver were given or human or animal figurines and these were either buried or hung on the walls of the shrine.

After the official sacrifices, personal offerings could be accepted and divided between the idol and the priests for their up-keep. These private offerings included specially prepared food, chicha, beads, feathers and ground or carved shells. Sometimes individual offerings consisted of blood from the lobes of ears or a few eyebrow hairs or eyelashes.

Sacrifices to the Sun were performed daily in the main square of Cuzco. Before sunrise a fire of carved wood was laid and lit just as the Sun rose. Specially prepared food was thrown in for the Sun to eat and the priests consumed the surplus. Later in the day a dark red llama was sacrificed and some baskets of coca were burned with it. Other sacrifices were made on the first day of every month when the emperor and his court gathered in the main square. Here 100 llamas were dedicated by the high priest to Viracocha in the name of the Sun. Then they were divided between thirty attendants, representing the days of the month, each of whom had to bring out in turn during the month his share of four llamas for sacrifice. At the end of the month the sacrificed llamas were cut into quarters and burned as completely as possible. The unburned bones were ground into a powder, a little of which

At Cuzco a Christian church stands not only on the site but on the surviving lower walls of the Inca Temple of the Sun.

the priests blew from their hands while they repeated a ritual phrase. The remaining powder was stored.

The Incas believed that virtuous people went to live in the 'upper world' or *Janaq Pacha* which was very much like the earth, with rivers, animals and gods in direct communication with earth. The Christian idea of heaven is similar, but Janaq Pacha is conceived in more detail. Sinners went to the 'lower world' or *Uku Pacha* where they only had stones for food and suffered from cold and hunger. The nobility were believed to go to Janaq Pacha whether or not they were virtuous. The souls of the dead might linger on earth and protect their descendants. They needed offerings of food and liked to have their bodies brought out to take part in festivals. The Incas and almost all the other peoples of Peru do not appear to have believed in the reincarnation of the body.

Conclusions

All ancient Peruvians seem to have believed in some sort of after-life as evidenced by their burying food, drink and personal possessions with the dead. The sun, moon and stars featured in varying degrees of importance in their beliefs. In particular it was important for them to observe the movements of the heavens to know when to plant their crops.

Animals formed an integral part of the religion of ancient Peru. On the one hand there were beasts like llamas which were sacrificed on special occasions. On the other there were jaguars and pumas, often provided with human attributes, which appear to have been deified. It is often difficult to say exactly what role these felines occupied in religion and mythology. They may just have been legendary monsters, like the dragon which was killed by St. George.

The creation legends of the Titicaca area and of the Incas have characteristics, such as a flood, in common with those of other peoples like the Greeks. Also some of the acts of Viracocha were very similar to those of Jesus Christ. This may partly explain why Christianity was able to take root after the Spanish conquest.

Chapter VII Craftsmanship

In pre-Spanish Peru there seems to have been some division between objects made just for use, such as cooking pots, and those made to be looked at, such as elaborately modelled and painted portrait jars. The same can be said of textiles, metalwork and stone carving where as many utility as non-utility items have come to light. Architecture covered the range from normal domestic buildings to temples. We do not know whether the ancient Peruvians had developed an abstract concept of art as it exists nowadays in western Europe and North America. However, there is a considerable quantity of ancient material which is classified as art by modern art historians although it is strictly 'applied' art such as pottery, textiles and metalwork. There was no painting on canvas in pre-Spanish Peru, although walls were sometimes painted with murals.

Textiles

The most abundant remains of Peruvian textiles have been found in tombs and refuse deposits on the coast where the preservation conditions are good. The earliest of these date to about 4500 BC. Fine textile-making developed in ancient Peru due to a combination of several factors. First, there were excellent fibres available from both animal and plant sources. Secondly, the daily as well as seasonal fluctuations in temperature in all areas made warm clothing necessary, particularly so in the high Andes. Finally, the development and success of irrigation agriculture and the rich fishing on the coast brought in regular surpluses of food and allowed the leisure time in which fine and complex fabrics might be created. The largest and most elaborate textiles were made during the first millenium BC, by the Paracas people.

The ancient Peruvians used almost every known technique of modern weaving as well as several which are either impractical or impossible for mechanical looms. They were highly skilled in both spinning and dyeing,

Backstrap looms (above) like those seen in the central highlands and on the coast today (left) produced most of the cloth that has been recovered from ancient Peruvian sites. The warp is stretched from one cross-bar slung from a post to another attached to a belt which the weaver sits in. Anything wider than a man's arm-span must have been made on a different loom. An upright variety is recorded from Inca times.

The first textiles in Peru were cotton and one of the earliest designs (below) has been made out on a scrap of cloth dating from about 2000 BC. But wool, particularly alpaca wool, was soon also in use (right).

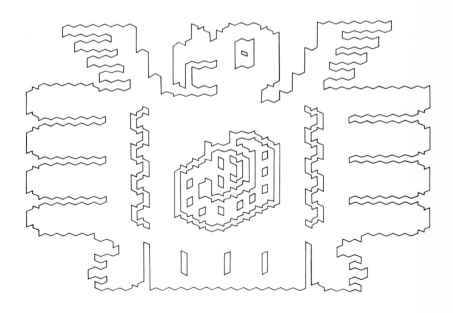

being able to produce a large range of colours. Great pride was taken in weaving and many of the remaining examples are of excellent quality.

The main fibre used in the earliest Peruvian textiles was cotton. Studies by Junius Bird of the textiles in refuse deposits in the Chicama and Virú valleys left by people who knew neither maize nor pottery have shown that cotton was the principal fibre. He also found that bast (the inner bark of a tree) was sometimes blended or plied with it. Twisted sedge (a kind of reed) was used to make open-mesh coiled pouches and mats. Recent work at Early Preceramic sites on the central coast has shown that sedge and bast were mainly used to make nets, bags and mats. Cotton was almost exclusively used for textiles, especially clothes and shrouds.

Analysis of the Paracas textiles has shown that the earlier ones, belonging to the Cavernas tombs, contained more cotton than wool as compared with the later Necropolis material. Old mummy wrappings from Supé and Ancón are all made from cotton except for one piece in which a little wool is used. All the evidence points to cotton being the oldest fibre used in Peruvian textiles.

In Inca times vicuña wool was supposed to have been used only for the Inca himself and the nobility. However, research carried out by Mr Truman Bailey suggests that many of the finer wool fabrics which were previously classed as vicuña are in fact of selected alpaca wool. Vicuña wool is more difficult to spin than that of the alpaca since, in the words of the spinners, 'the vicuña is a very active playful animal' and its wool retains these characteristics.

The ancient Peruvians were skilled at dyeing and produced a wide range of colours. Analysis has distinguished 190 separate hues in the Paracas Necropolis dyed yarns, some of which are the result of uneven fading, but the great majority of which are genuinely different. Most of these would have been obtained from plants. In addition, the cochineal insect was no doubt an important source of dye.

Very little is known of the dyeing process. Mordants (substances which fixed colouring matter) such as alum were used and permanent brilliant colours were produced. Raw stocks of cotton were dyed but rarely those of wool. Cones of dyed blue cotton prepared for spinning have been found in Peruvian work baskets. Junius Bird noted the survival of this practice in 1947 in the Chicama Valley. He found that the cotton was dyed with the seeds still attached and, when dry, the fibres could be handled just as easily as dyed cotton.

There are some archaeological clues to the dates when different dyes were first introduced. The only dye applied to the Preceramic textiles found in the Chicama Valley by Junius Bird was blue. At Supé and Ancón in Chavín times a little red dye has been found in addition to the blue. On Paracas Cavernas textiles there were ten or twelve colours while on the Necropolis examples the range of colours reached its maximum.

The oldest textiles tend to have rather coarse and uneven yarns. In the refuse in which they occur in the Chicama Valley no recognizable spindles and no spindle whorls have been found, only thousands of wood fragments and twigs. Junius Bird has pointed out that in the same valley today women are sometimes seen twisting coarse yarn, using an unworked straight shoot of a local shrub for a spindle. Women probably did most of the spinning in antiquity. When making coarse yarn these spindles are used without a whorl (the fly of a spindle). The lower ends are held all the time and twisted by the fingers of the right hand while the left draws and lays the fibres from a bunch of cotton tied to the end of a distaff (the staff to which and from which the thread is drawn to be spun by the spindle).

Between Preceramic times and the Spanish conquest spinning was developed to produce yarns considerably finer than those made by modern machines using the same staples. Delicate spindles of thorn and wood, equipped with tiny whorls, were used to spin fine yarns. When the spindle was in use the lower end rested in a special cup of pottery, wood or gourd which minimized vibration and strain, essential for spinning fine cotton. This method is still in use but the spindles are more crude and the yarn produced is heavier.

There is little information about the use of distaffs. At the time of the Inca empire a forked stick was used. Some more carefully made slotted wooden distaffs, one with wool still in place, have been found. Some modern spinners have a roll of prepared wool or cotton looped round the left wrist and hand, and draw out and lay the fibres with the left fingers, while the right hand operates the spindle and stretches the fibres as the spinning progresses. Another modern method involves fastening a bunch of prepared cotton to the end of a reed, some 127 centimetres long, which is held between the left arm and the body, leaving both hands free to manipulate the fibres. A simple distaff like this may have been used to hold the conical bunches of prepared cotton that are often found in work baskets of the Late Intermediate Period.

Most of the textiles excavated from tombs and refuse deposits were made on backstrap looms, like modern ones used in the central highlands and on the coast. This type of loom consists of two sticks, called loom bars, with the warp (threads stretched lengthwise in a loom to be crossed by the weft) stretched between them. The upper bar is suspended from a post or other support, while the lower, tied to a belt passing behind the weaver's back, rests above the lap. As work progresses on a long fabric, the warp is unrolled from the upper bar and the finished fabric is rolled on to the lower.

When these looms are warped the yarn was, and still is, wound with a figure-of-eight motion between two stakes. This figure-of-eight crossing, termed the lease, automatically separates the alternate turns. Once the yarn has been warped off, it is laced fast to the loom bars so that, when completed, all four edges of the fabric are uniformly finished off.

The backstrap loom has the disadvantage that a single person cannot weave a fabric wider than the working span of the arms. The length is limited by the amount of cloth that can be rolled and supported on the lower bar. On average the maximum width seems to be about 76 centimetres. The large Paracas cloths with widths up to 5 metres and lengths of 26 metres were probably woven on some other type of loom. A super backstrap loom of roughly three times the normal size and operated by three women working as a team has been recorded in modern Peru by Truman Bailey. This version would be more restricted in the length it could produce than the width.

A type of loom which stood upright was also used in Inca times. It consisted of a vertical frame of four poles built against a wall. This machine was used to make a wide colourful and ornate cloth called cumbi which was originally made in the tapestry technique.

Dress and decoration

Evidence for pre-Inca clothing comes mainly from tombs and from modelled and painted pots. In particular the pottery of the Moche people portrayed very vividly what they wore. Men usually had a loin cloth and a short sleeveless shirt underneath a tunic that ended above the knee and was fastened round the waist with a colourful woven belt. More important people appear to have had a large mantle. The legs and feet were usually bare and unshod but quite often the lower legs and feet were painted. The head was always covered (except if the person was a prisoner) and there was a great variety of headgear. The most common type was a turban wound round a small cap which was held in place by a strip of cloth that passed over the top and was tied under the chin. The back of the neck was usually covered by a cloth that fell over the back of the neck. The purpose of this was to keep the sun off the back of the head and neck and also to prevent sand from blowing in. Important people had head-dresses made from the skin of an animal, such as a puma, the head of which protruded from the front. Hats were sometimes decorated with small pieces of metal or feathers.

Moche women, not frequently depicted on pots, tended to be less ornately dressed than men, their main item of clothing consisting of a loose tunic which reached to the knee. The head was either bare or covered with a piece of cloth.

Ornamentation ranged from painting the skin, especially the face and legs, to the wearing of jewellery. Some kind of tattooing seems to have been used. Men had ornaments for the nose, ears and lips. Nose ornaments were generally in the shape of a disc or crescent. Ear-rings, sometimes in gold, usually consisted of cylindrical bars which ended in discs up to 15 centimetres in diameter. The neck was often adorned with large collars of stone beads or precious metal and bracelets were worn on the arms and forearms and there were also ornaments for legs.

170

Sandal, cap and tunic (below) of the Peruvian Indian in pre-Spanish times have all been found in one form or another by the archaeologists and are matched by the costume recorded on the ancient pottery (above).

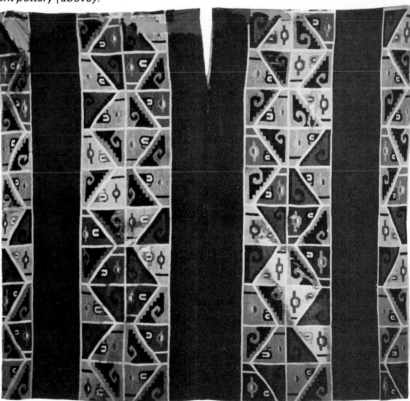

171

The difference between male and female costume, evident from Moche pots, has also been noted on one Nazca vessel. This depicts a man wearing a turban-like head-dress while the women are bare headed. The man is dressed in a shirt and short breeches while the women wear long tunics.

Chimú pottery and textiles show a continuation of Moche clothing styles in a less elaborate form, although this may partly be explained by the relative lack of painting and modelling on Chimú pots. Men continued to wear shirts which appear to have been fairly long and may have had short sleeves; but the evidence for the latter is rather scant. Headgear consisted of large-sized ornamented head-dresses for festivals and simpler turban-like attire for everyday wear. The ornamented head-dresses often had half-moon top-knots which may have been made from feathers. Certainly some fine featherwork, including head-dresses, dating to the Chimú period has been found in tombs. On textiles feathers are usually attached to a frame or ring of basketwork.

Inca clothing in the highlands needed to be warm and much of it was made from alpaca wool, some of it from llama wool. However, on the coast Inca administrators used cotton, a cooler fabric for these warmer regions.

From the age of puberty, when he was about fourteen, the ordinary man wore a loin cloth about 15 centimetres wide which passed between the legs and over a narrow belt front and back, with the ends hanging part of the way down the thighs. Over the loin cloth was worn a sleeveless tunic of a long piece of cloth with a slit in the middle for the head. This cloth hung to just above the knees and was doubled over like a sack, with the sides sewn up leaving spaces at the top for the arms. An ankle-length tunic was worn on certain ceremonial occasions. Fine tunics were usually decorated with colourful geometric motifs, but the usual design consisted of an inverted triangle at the neck and a broad band around the waist and lower edge. Much Inca ornamentation consisted of squares arranged in rows which were either left plain or filled with little, constantly recurring designs.

Over the tunic men wore a large cloak measuring about 190 by 150 centimetres. It was made from two strips of cloth sewn together up the middle like the mantles worn by Indian women today. It was either tied over one shoulder to leave an arm free or thrown over the shoulders with two corners tied over the chest. During violent exercise or at work the cloak was removed.

Inca women wore a long dress, secured at the waist by a wide sash, and a mantle similar to the one worn by the men. They wore no undergarments. The dress consisted of a rectangular piece of cloth wound round the body under the arms, with the edges overlapping on one side and the top edges pulled up and fastened with straight pins over the shoulders. The skirt reached down to the ankles. Over the dress a large mantle was thrown over the shoulders and fastened on to the chest with a large pin or *topu*. The latter was made of gold, silver, copper or bronze, according to the status of

A man's sleeveless woollen tunic from Inca days. ▶

the wearer, and its head was beaten out flat and perforated for small bells or coloured threads. The sash securing the dress was decorated with designs arranged in squares.

Both sexes wore sandals of untanned leather, made from the neck of a llama, with woollen fastenings. In wet weather this untanned leather became soft and had to be discarded. There were various other types of footwear within the Inca empire so that, for example, the Aymara in the south sometimes wore moccasins instead of sandals. The Incas wore fringed leg bands below the knees but no other leg coverings.

Among the Incas the men wore most of the ornaments since these denoted rank and status. All men of royal lineage and 'Incas by privilege' wore largely cylindrical ear plugs of gold, wood or other material pierced through the ear lobes with the large round end facing outwards. The highest officials wore wide bracelets of gold and silver. Feathers were used as collars or as ornamentation in head-dresses or woven into clothing for special occasions. Women usually only wore bone beads or shell pins and necklaces. Flowers are often associated with women's dress and women are shown carrying them.

Pottery

The ancient Peruvians were highly skilled potters even though their technology did not include the potter's wheel or any knowledge of glazes. Even today fine pots are still made by using traditional pre-Spanish techniques.

It is possible that the manufacture of pottery was introduced into Peru from elsewhere, such as north-west South America. The earliest pottery found in Peru dates to about 1800 BC and its quality is good, certainly not what one would expect from people making their first experiments in its manufacture. The earliest pottery in South America that has been found so far dates to about 3000 BC and was excavated on the Caribbean coast of Colombia. However, it remains possible that the local antecedents for Peruvian pottery will be found within that country.

The ancient Peruvian potter's technique can be reconstructed from study of the archaeological specimens and comparison with modern methods. Detailed studies have not yet been made of the sources of the clay available in antiquity but clay suitable for pottery occurs today in most of the coastal valleys and highland basins. Recently a study by Christopher Donnan of modern potters in the Callejón de Huaylas has shown that they will sometimes take prepared clay to distant communities and make pottery to order on the spot. This avoids transporting whole vessels which might break in transit.

Once the clay has been prepared, by soaking, kneading and pounding, a grit temper is added to make it more workable, less liable to crack as it dries and better able to withstand the sudden temperature changes of simple firing methods. Tempering materials depend on what is available and the type of pottery to be made but in antiquity they included crushed stone and potsherds, sand, mica and shell. For modelled and decorated pottery a fine sand was used on the north coast while the coarser cooking and storage vessels from that area have particles of gravel in their temper.

The method used for shaping the early pottery depended to some extent on the desired size and also upon the technology available in a given area at any particular time. Also several techniques could be used to make one vessel. Coiling was extensively used but the marks of the coils were usually smoothed out. In other instances a lump of clay was prepared and then modelled into the desired form. Both methods were either done completely by hand or with the aid of a wooden 'paddle' while the inner surface of the growing pot was supported by an 'anvil' of stone or some other material. The paddle and anvil technique is still used on the north coast of Peru. In both methods the base of the vessel generally rests on a large potsherd or slightly concave pottery plate which enables the potter to rotate the clay as it is worked.

The Moche and later north-coast peoples were noted for their use of moulds to shape pottery. These were made from fired clay and were formed over an actual object, like an ear of corn, or an existing pottery vessel. Moist clay was pressed into the moulds and, as the clay began to dry and shrink away from the inside of the mould it could easily be removed. Although one-piece moulds were sometimes used, two-piece moulds were the most common. By looking at broken pots one can see that their different sections were joined up after removal from the moulds and that handles, spouts and some ornaments were made separately and then added. Moulding was usually employed for the non-functional pottery, particularly what was intended to represent daily life or mythology. The characteristic stirrup spout bottles often had chambers which were largely mould-made but which had been finished off with several coils of clay. Large vessels for everyday use were made by coiling and the paddle and anvil technique.

Decoration varied with the area and period of manufacture. In Early Horizon times many designs were incised, stamped or modelled. Rocker stamping (a series of indentations made by rocking a shell backwards and forwards in the wet clay) was used to produce a contrasting pattern between areas already decorated with incised lines. These techniques were especially used on pottery from Chavín de Huantar. Towards the end of the Early Horizon ceramic paints began to be used in Peru. A type of pottery found both at Chavín and on the north coast (known as Wacheqsa at Chavín and as Cupisnique Transitorio on the north coast) was decorated with a silvery-black graphite paint applied to cover zones which were frequently bounded by narrow incisions made when the paste was dry. On the south coast, in the Ica-Nazca area, the incised details were coloured after firing with

176

The wheel and thus wheel-thrown pottery were unknown in ancient Peru. But potters were skilled in a wide range of all other techniques, including the use of a one-piece mould (above), polychrome painting (right top), negative painting (right centre) and modelling (right bottom). The modelled man is himself burnishing the surface of a pot. One of the many less ornamental vessels that must also have been called for is a storage jar of the Moche period that was recently found in the Moche area today (below).

powdered mineral pigments mixed with resins to form a lacquer-like coating.

During the Early Intermediate and later periods some vessels, once shaped and smoothed, were coated with a clay wash or slip, consisting of a suspension of fine clay in water, in order to provide a certain colour or a finer surface or form a base for painted decoration. Paints were made from pigments and clays suspended in water. The total range of colours that could be made by this method was small. Moche pottery was often decorated with slips and pigments made like this and the colours were usually limited to red and white.

As glazes were not used polishing or rubbing the vessel surface to give it lustre was the most usual means of obtaining a fine finish, such as on Moche or Nazca pottery. The two main polishing tools seem to have been a smooth hard stone or a bone implement. On Moche and Nazca pottery the stroke marks can rarely be seen so that the polishing was probably done when the vessels were nearly dry. Stroke marks can be largely removed by rubbing the vessel with the hand or a soft cloth. Usually only painted areas were polished, especially on Moche pots.

It is quite likely that almost all ancient Peruvian pottery was made in open fires rather than in kilns; no examples of ancient kilns have been found by archaeologists and modern traditional potters often use the open-fire method. In north Peru the same modern potters stack the pots one on top of another in an open pit and then surround them with fuel. Oxidized wares must have been achieved in ancient times, as they are today, by arranging the fuel and unfired pottery so that almost all the carbon present burned away in the open fire. Most of the clay used contained iron compounds which, when oxidized as ferric oxide, produced colours in the pottery ranging from cream to red, depending on the amount of oxide present. If the same clays are fired to the same temperatures without oxygen, they may end up light to dark grey or even bluish because the iron compounds will be reduced to ferrous oxide. However, many grey and blackware Peruvian pots have obtained their colouring from retained or absorbed carbon rather than by reduction. Grey and black can be obtained simply by smothering the fire with organic material like grass or leaves or just earth before all the carbon in the fuel has been burned. Black fireclouds are found on the chambers of redware vessels and these black patches are almost certainly the result of that section of the vessel being covered with unburnt fuel.

One decorative technique used after firing, mainly found on Recuay- and Gallinazo-style pots from north Peru, was 'negative painting'. This method has been reconstructed by Robert Sonin, an American archaeologist. A design is first painted on a fired 'oxidized' vessel using a fine fluid mixture of clay. When the clay is firm it forms a 'resist' and protects the surface underneath it. The exposed areas of the vessel can then be blackened by smoking or they can be coated with various water soluble substances

A 'stirrup spout' bottle of about 800 BC in Early
Horizon times has shell stamping on its body and
incised lines round the base (right). A burnished
Chimú pot (above) shows Inca influence of the
15th century AD in the flared rim of its spout.

Sheet silver and gold soldered together to make a spoon and rattle of about 800 BC (above); an embossed Nazca gold mask of about AD 500 (left); a hammered copper mask of Moche workmanship, also of about AD 500 (below); and a Chimú knife of arsenic bronze (bottom left).

which, when held over a fire, will char and deposit carbon on the surface. The clay resist peels off to reveal a carbon negative image of the design. Since the carbon on the 'field' of the design is easily burnt away the technique is never found on cooking pots.

Sometimes a black pigment was applied to vessels for decoration. This was especially true for some Moche pottery; here the pigment seems to have been an organic liquid which was painted on the vessels after they were fired. These were then heated to scorch the substance on to the surface. Moche potters only applied this organic black to vessels coloured with red or white pigments; the black served simply to increase elaboration and detail.

There has been some speculation that stirrup spout bottles, common on the north coast of Peru for 1500 years before the Spanish conquest, were made for use as water bottles rather than simply as ornaments in the manner of Chelsea porcelain figures in England. However the stirrup form makes the pouring of water very difficult. Also, the chamber is likely to break away if a heavy weight of water is put into it and if the vessel is picked up by the handle only. Some double-chambered vessels have a whistle which can be made to work by partially filling both chambers with water and then tilting the whole pot. Broken pieces of stirrup spout pots and other fine modelled and painted vessels have been found in domestic refuse. This suggests that this fine pottery was kept in people's houses during the lifetime of their owners, some getting broken in the course of events, and that it was not made especially for burial.

For cooking, wide-mouthed pots were made and jars with necks of varying sizes and shapes were used for storage. Cooking and storage pots were usually undecorated although occasionally, such as on Gallinazo pottery, designs were incised and indented on them. Sometimes Moche potters would put incised marks on plain-ware vessels to identify them during the firing process. These marks usually took the form of a few short lines, a cross or a simple pattern placed on one side of the neck of a jar.

Metallurgy

The earliest metalwork found in Peru dates to the latter part of the Early Horizon. It consists of Cupisnique-style gold objects from three tombs in the Lambayeque Valley on the north coast. They include crowns, circlets, ear spools, finger rings, necklaces, pins, spoons and tweezers, all made of sheet gold except for two specimens which are partly of gold and partly of silver. The Early Horizon metalsmiths could not only hammer gold in sheets but could also decorate it by embossing (making raised designs), champlevé (driving in the background of a design) and by various combinations of these. They also discovered annealing, making it possible to soften the metal and thus hammer it into more elaborate forms. They joined sheets of metal or the parts of hollow figurines and beads by soldering. However their metal technology did not include moulding and casting and they did not know the use of copper, lead, tin or alloys, or the arts of gilding and silvering.

On the south coast towards the end of the Early Horizon the Paracas people had beaten gold ornaments which were embossed. Also they could anneal metal. Later, in Early Intermediate times, the Nazca people had articles of sheet gold like masks, head ornaments, large nose pendants, cut-out figures to be sewn on clothing, and hollow beads. Embossing at this time was probably carried out by placing a stone of suitable shape under the gold sheet as it was beaten out over a piece of wood.

During the Early Intermediate Period metal technology was more advanced on the north than on the south coast. By about the first half of the Christian era the simple casting of copper was being carried out in the Viru-Chicama area. In addition to copper there is some evidence that the Moche used arsenic bronze. They developed casting by the lost wax or *cire-perdu* method. They also soldered and could weld. Gold was used as a setting for other materials so that, for example, gold ear spools were inlaid with turquoise and shell. Some head-dresses were made of repoussé gold and had cut-out designs attached with gold wires.

By the end of the Middle Horizon copper-tin bronze was being used in the highlands of south Peru and on the Bolivian altiplano. The source of the tin was cassiterite and an oxide of that metal was plentiful in Bolivia and northern Argentina both as placer deposits (an alluvial deposit containing minerals in particles) and in veins.

In contrast, north Peru, from the end of the Middle Horizon until the Inca conquest, developed and used arsenic bronze. In addition an alloy of copper and silver was used in the north to manufacture certain kinds of objects made of sheet metal. The two bronzes developed side by side and some recent analyses by Heather Lechtman, an American metallurgist, have shown that copper-tin bronze was used in the north in the latter part of the Late Intermediate Period.

In the Inca period copper-tin bronze was extensively used. A study of Inca bronze from Machu Picchu showed that the Inca metalsmiths had complete control of the properties of that metal. Bronzes, of a high tin content, usually between 10 per cent and 13 per cent tin, were the strongest alloys and used in castings. Bronzes of a low tin content, about 5 per cent tin, were used for forged objects like axes, chisels, tweezers, *tumis*, topus and the like since these alloys were ductile and easily worked without becoming brittle. Copper-tin bronze became the all-purpose metal in the southern Andes during the Late Intermediate Period and the Late Horizon. It was used for both utilitarian and ceremonial objects rather like stainless steel is used in industrial countries today. Also it replaced the arsenic-bronze which had been made in the Chimú empire before the Inca conquest. This replacement may well have been a political act, tightening political control with the imposition of Inca technology.

182

Its cane framework thatched with junco grass, a house of about 3400 BC has been found at Chilca on the central coast of Peru (top left). A recent shelter (top right) is built along the same lines. A house of about AD 500 on the coast would have been built of mud-brick or stone and left open to the cooling sea breezes (above). A highland house of about AD 1400 was probably of stone and is shown with a steep thatched roof that would drain off heavy rains (right).

One technique used by the Chimú to make their metal objects appear to be gold was depletion gilding. In the formation of a sheet of an alloy of copper and gold, for example, annealing to relax the metal causes the copper to oxidise on the surface which, as more copper diffuses to the surface and oxidises, is depleted in metallic copper. Once enough has been lost the object appears golden through the formation of a surface layer. Chimú objects, like large mummy masks as much as 70 centimetres across, were made from a ternary alloy of copper, silver and gold whose surfaces they treated to deplete them of copper and silver and thereby to enrich them in gold. Much of the sheet gold manufactured in the Chimú empire was made from this alloy which can, according to Heather Lechtman, contain concentrations of gold as low as 12 per cent by weight. She analysed the metal gilt of a Chimú mummy mask from Batan Grande in the Lambayeque Valley and found that it was made of a ternary alloy of copper, silver and gold, with a gold content of about 40 per cent by weight. On this example there were some traces of red paint and also holes through which decorative appendages could have been secured. Lechtman's work on gilding has led her to suggest that many of the large gold objects that impressed the Spaniards in Cuzco and other places, such as gold plates on walls, and gardens made of gold birds, animals and trees, were not made of gold but of a ternary copper-silver-gold alloy. The fabled ransom of Atahualpa which Pizarro had melted down may have been made largely from this alloy rather than from solid gold.

The Spaniards left descriptions of mining methods in the Inca empire. Most gold seems to have been obtained by washing gravel from stream beds rather than by mining. Most of the silver was extracted in the form of native silver from pits and from smelting ores. One description of Inca gallery mines in Bolivia relates how they had no light and were only broad enough for one person at a time to enter crouching down. Other mines were like wells a man's height in depth so that the worker could just throw the earth from below to the ground surface.

Blowpipes and furnaces were used to melt metal. Garcilaso de la Vega relates how the Peruvian Indians blew down copper tubes which were almost completely blocked at the other end, having only one small hole through which the compressed air escaped with great force. Wind furnaces or *huayras* were used to smelt silver and also to process copper and lead ores. These furnaces were described by Baltazar Ramirez in 1597 as being portable and shaped like a pot made of crude clay. They were about a metre high and had a width of a third of a metre at the base, increasing to half a metre at the top. They were filled with burning charcoal and placed in exposed windy places. The front of the furnace was full of holes through which the wind blew to heat up the fire and melt the ore on top of it. At the back and sides were a few other small holes to let out the smoke. The metal, such as a mixture of silver and lead impurities, dripped into a crude clay bowl at the foot of the furnace. Pure silver was refined in special furnaces.

Mud-bricks (above) and stone (below) were used for building in ancient Peru according to availability. Bricks were built up in columns (above) or in layers. Stone was often unbonded (below left), masonry being brought to a fine art by the Incas (below right).

The buildings erected in pre-Spanish Peru usually made use of locally available materials such as stone and earth. The round arch appears to have been unknown although Larco Hoyle has claimed that some Moche tombs had rounded arches to support their roofs. Since Peru is a major earthquake region all buildings had to take account of this. It is often remarked that in Cuzco the Spanish colonial and more modern buildings suffer moderate to severe damage in earthquakes. In contrast the Inca walls, built without mortar so that the stones are bonded into each other, suffer little or no harm. In the Chimú capital of Chan Chan exterior and some interior walls of the cuidadelas are wider at the base than at the top and the adobe bricks are bigger at the bottom. In the major earthquake of May, 1970, these walls stood up well while modern ones nearby, built untapered with the same size brick all the way up, collapsed.

A well-preserved example of an early house put up in Preceramic times is that excavated and also reconstructed by Christopher Donnan in 1963 at the site of Chilca on the central coast. This structure is dated by radiocarbon to about 3400 BC, which makes it the earliest artificial shelter reported from Peru. Its shape was conical and resembled a beehive. It had been partially dug into the ground to a depth of about 35 centimetres and the floor was packed earth. Cane was used to make much of the frame of the house and the cane stalks were tied together with *junco*, rope made from junco grass (a kind of rush) and still widely used in Peru. The door was made by tying a hoop of grass to two of the original frame pieces and a cross brace. In order to prevent the lower part of the house, which was below ground level, from collapsing inwards braces of whalebone and wood were inserted round the frame and into the ground. When the frame was completed it was covered with junco grass which was probably held on to the part of the frame above ground by junco rope.

There does not seem to have been anything more than a simple opening for a door in the Chilca house. As no hearth or ashes were found inside the house cooking was probably done outside. The purpose of the house was probably just to provide shelter from the cold and a place to sleep. Two of Donnan's Peruvian assistants had, when they were young, either lived in similar structures or had seen them being made by others. Similar structures are also often built on small Peruvian farms for use as temporary shelters during such periods as harvest.

None of the domestic or ceremonial structures of the ancient Peruvians appear to have had chimneys. Even today in the Andes the Indians just allow the smoke to escape through the doorway. The most vivid record of the ancient houses are the modelled pots made by the Moche. Smaller dwellings are shown with one entrance but no door just like some Indian houses today. For ventilation there appear to have been vents on either side of the house, below a slanting roof which was probably turned towards the sea to get the full effect of the sea breezes. Remains of Moche houses positioned to receive the sea breezes have been found on hillside terraces. Excavations by the author in 1970 inside a Moche house located between the Moche and Chicama valleys revealed a low earth bench which was probably used as a bed just as similar ones are still used by highland Indians. The lower walls of this house were made of stones gathered from a nearby river bed while the upper sections could have been partially open to give ventilation. Modelled pots suggest that the walls of some Moche houses were plastered with mud and may have been vividly painted on the outside. However the only surviving Moche murals are those from temple structures like Pañamarca in the Nepeña Valley.

The temples of the Moche were usually large terraced mounds, such as the Huaca del Sol, made of adobe bricks which were generally rectangular but lacked standardized dimensions, even though they were made in moulds. Most of the adobes used to build the Huacas Sol and Luna were made from a brown water-laid silt found nearby. The moulds were probably made from smooth slats, for they produced bricks with flat sides. Some had makers' marks, such as a diagonal line or a circle, impressed on the top surfaces before the mud had dried. Since there was no writing actual names could not be inscribed. The Huaca del Sol appears to have been built up as a series of unbonded adobe-brick columns. In contrast the Huaca de la Luna was built in at least three and possibly five layers, one of which had been covered with white plaster. This layered construction, like the marzipan and icing on a Christmas cake, has also been discovered at the Moche pyramid of Huancaco in the Virú Valley. The various layers of the Luna appear to have been built without any significant time-lag between them. One possible explanation for this method is that it was the result of work done by different groups of people performing a sort of labour tax.

Chan Chan

Large cities were built on the coast of Peru between about AD 1000 and the Inca conquest in about AD 1470. The most notable of these was the Chimú capital of Chan Chan, the central part of which is estimated to have covered over 24 square kilometres. The main architectural units of the city consist of ten large enclosures or ciudadelas that are arranged in a sort of broken rectangle round the centre of the site. The overall layout of these buildings and the city as a whole suggests that it was gradually built over a period of between two and three hundred years. Each ciudadela seems to have functioned as a palace for the current ruler of Chan Chan, with each building himself a new one. Therefore if ten ciudadelas were each occupied for a period of about 25 years, it is likely that the first one was built about AD 1200 and the tenth one finished about AD 1450. Each ciudadela is roughly rectangular in plan and has its main entrance in the north wall. The exterior

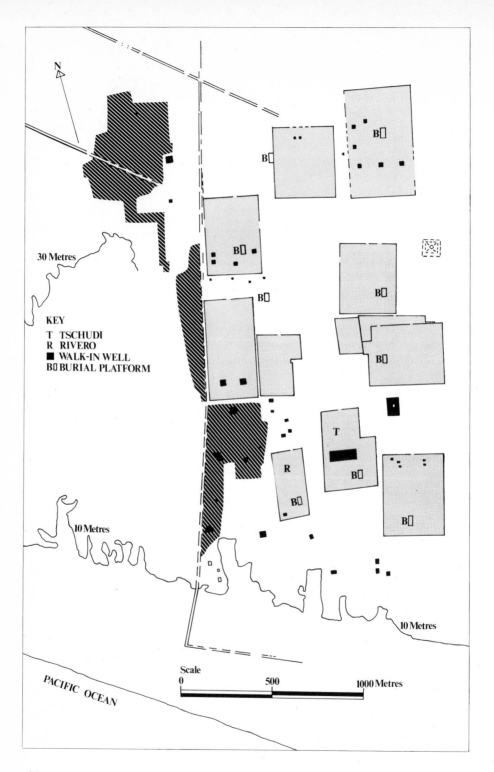

N

30 Metres

KEY

T TSCHUDI
R RIVERO
■ WALK-IN WELL
B⬚ BURIAL PLATFORM

B⬚

B⬚

B⬚

B⬚

B⬚

B⬚

T

R

B⬚

B⬚

B⬚

B⬚

10 Metres

10 Metres

Scale
0   500   1000 Metres

PACIFIC OCEAN

188

Notable among several large cities built on the coast of Peru between about AD 1000 and 1476 was Chan Chan, the Chimú capital (left). Covering some 24 square kilometres overlooking the sea, it was dominated by the rectangular palace enclosures of the kingdom's successive rulers. Each one included a burial platform (top right), a water supply (centre right) and lavishly decorated rooms (below). Hatched areas on the plan show where commoners' dwellings have been found.

walls now have a maximum height of 8 to 9 metres but Kent Day estimates that they could have been from 10 to 12 metres high in their heyday. They were not fortified but provided privacy, and shelter from the sea breezes. Generally they had a stone foundation on top of which the largest sun-dried adobe bricks were placed. Above these, smaller adobes were often laid in layers coated with mud mortar which ran alternately along and then across the line of the wall. The wall was thus bonded by alternate rows of bricks, termed 'runners and headers', separated by mud layers. Kent Day found that many of the adobes used were irregular in size but had an overall tiered effect. In contrast to the Huaca del Sol, none of those used at Chan Chan had any makers' marks on them. The general impression is that the Chan Chan bricks were mass-produced by unskilled workers. They were probably made locally since there is quite an amount of grit in them which looks as if it has come from alluvial deposits in the neighbourhood of the city. The exterior walls seem to have been divided into horizontal and near-vertical sections, each of which was probably allowed to dry before another was added. Day points out that, if the whole height was built at one go, the wet mud and mortar which coated the layers of adobes would cause the completed wall to slump. He also found that there were examples of poor quality workmanship in the construction of some walls which again points to the use of unskilled workers.

Inside each ciudadela are the remains of courtyards, storerooms, U-shaped reception rooms called *audiencias*, corridors, kitchen areas and burial platforms. In addition, each has some sort of water supply, such as a well with a ramp down which people could walk to fill up their vessels. Recent excavations by Kent Day in ciudadela Rivero uncovered remains of wooden algarroba posts in corridors where they probably supported the roof frame. He discovered that the roof frames were made from cane that had been bound and wrapped with reed fibre twine and were covered with grass and earth which was quite an adequate cover since it rained very infrequently. Some roofs were flat or slightly tilted, needing support from wooden columns, while others were gable-ended and appear not to have had interior supports beneath their span. Some of the interior walls were covered with low-relief murals made from mud plaster.

The ordinary inhabitants of Chan Chan, who probably built the ciudadelas, appear to have lived mainly in small dwellings along the western edge of the central part of the city. Rooms in the houses were irregularly shaped and clustered together. The foundations seem to have been mainly of field stones or adobe bricks but never seem to have been more than half a metre high. The superstructures were made of reed mats suspended on cane-pole frameworks. A similar method of construction is used in *estera* mat houses found today on the coast of Peru. Food and other items were stored in pits, or in bins under the floor or in buried or sunken pots.

A Peruvian Indian in pre-Spanish times. ▶

Inca building

Inca public buildings, such as the Temples of the Sun, or the palaces of the Inca emperors or fortresses were built by the government to plans made by professional architects who were exempt from ordinary taxation. Labour was provided by the mit'a. Designs for buildings, roads, terraces and towns were worked out on models that were usually made of clay but sometimes of stone. Measurements were probably made with a sliding ruler consisting of two sticks which were moved along parallel with one another until their combined lengths exactly covered the space to be measured.

In the highlands the main Inca buildings were built wholly or partly of stone. The stone was generally worked with stone hammers while sand and water were probably used for polishing. In Cuzco Yucay limestone, a hard grey stone cut into polygonal blocks by Inca masons, or diorite porphyry, a green stone used in large polygonal blocks or a black andesite, which weathers to a chocolate brown colour, were the three types used. The andesite, which was used in the Temple of the Sun and most Inca palaces, was brought from a distance since the nearest outcrop is about 14 kilometres from Cuzco. A large Inca stone block has been found near Ollantaytambo with the remains of wooden rollers underneath it, as if this were the means of transporting it, probably with the help of wooden levers and men pulling on ropes.

A notable feature of Inca masonry is that the edges of the blocks are bevelled so that the joints are emphasized, with the purely decorative effect of breaking up the wall surface into patterns of light and shade. The actual joints are usually so tight and true that it is difficult to put a pin into the crack. Although no mortar was used on the exterior face of the wall, in the interior the stones were rarely perfectly fitted and the cracks were filled with mud.

Quite a few Inca public buildings in and around Cuzco used adobe in their construction. In the early 1940s, when an adobe wall was being demolished in Cuzco, several courses of Inca adobe bricks were found in place on top of a stone wall. They had a high proportion of straw to mud, were roughly square in cross section and had a length of about 80 centimetres, which is rather long for adobe bricks. On the coast the Inca architects used mainly adobe but stone also appears as in the Mamacona at Pachacámac.

Inca roofs were thatched. Garcilaso de la Vega describes roofs in Inca times as 'made of poles fastened to each other transversely by strong cords. These supported a layer of grass of the thickness, in some of the houses, of six feet (183 centimetres) or more, which not only served for a cornice to the walls, but extended beyond them more than a yard (91·5 centimetres), as a pent-roof to keep the rain from the walls, and to shelter people beneath it. The part that projected beyond the walls was clipped very evenly. . . .' Some of these roofs lasted a long time and Squier describes one, that of the *Son-*

Inca walls at Machu Picchu, with a characteristic trapezoid opening and with bevelled edges emphasizing the precision of jointing in the masonry.

194

dorhuasi near lake Titicaca, which had survived for over 300 years. This example was actually in the form of a thatched dome on top of a circular building made from compacted clay.

Most Inca buildings were of a single storey with storage space under the roof although a number of two-storey and even three-storey ones have been found. In the last two examples each storey is placed directly over the one underneath and is not terraced. The trapezoid is a notable feature of late Inca architecture, after about AD 1470, and was used for all sizes of niches, doorways covered with stone or wooden lintels and for most of the windows. Even the silhouette of buildings was this shape since the walls sloped inward, with the heaviest masonry being at the base, probably placed there as an anti-seismic device. Although the corbel vault was known it was only used to roof small chambers. Sometimes architectural sculpture, usually in the form of pumas or snakes on the lintels of doorjambs, was used.

Inca houses were generally built in groups, each of which was surrounded by a wall with one entrance. Where the lie of the land allowed it the enclosures were usually rectangular. In the Inca village of Ollantaytambo up to six rectangular houses were arranged round the sides of an enclosure and faced an open court in the centre. The corners of the enclosures were often used for cooking or storage and sometimes were roofed. This kind of compound was probably the home of all the generations of an extended family. The enclosure walls were usually built of adobe or field stone but along the floors square blocks of earth were more commonly employed. In the highlands the houses only had one doorway which was closed by a curtain held in place by a stone when the owner was out. The few windows were small, since there was no glass, and the lack of chimneys or smoke-holes meant that house interiors were dark and smoky. Since the Indians spent most of their waking hours outside they did not really need comfortable houses.

There was hardly any furniture in an Inca house. A low clay stove with several holes in the top for the cooking pots and a small stoking hole at the front was the main item. A few irregular niches served as shelves while spare food and clothing was stored in large jars. Everyone slept in their clothes and most commoners just lay on the dirt floor in a long blanket. Nobles had a layer of straw or matting under the blanket to make it more comfortable.

Chapter VIII

**The Peruvian
Achievement**

When Pizarro and his companions landed on the coast of Peru in 1532 they discovered a remarkable civilization whose artistic achievements, many of which were then still buried in tombs, have been found to rival those of medieval Europe. The gold objects that Atahualpa ordered to be collected for Pizarro may well have mainly consisted of items which were not solid gold; they nevertheless represented a superb craft tradition. Without writing, the wheel or money the ancient Peruvians had developed an economic and political system within the Inca empire which ensured that nobody starved if their crops failed. The commoners did have to provide labour in the form of taxation through the mit'a and their movements were regulated but this was probably no more onerous than the burdens placed on medieval European serfs.

The Incas tried to give the impression that their empire was in fact entirely their own creation out of a state of chaos and barbarism that existed before. There is some truth in this, since, from about AD 1200 to 1438, the Incas had been just one of a number of small warring tribes in the Cuzco area. And archaeologists from Max Uhle onwards have shown that the Incas brought to a climax a long period of indigenous cultural development. Their great achievement was essentially one of good organization combined with military strength which enabled them to build up their empire in a space of about 40 years. In addition they were lucky in having two able emperors, Pachacuti and his son Topa Inca, who directed this expansion policy and also used diplomacy to avoid conflict and to persuade potential enemies to join them.

However, many of the great achievements of the Peruvian Indians were made before the Incas came to power. In particular, the Paracas weavers produced the most technically advanced textiles for over 1,000 years before anyone had even heard of the Incas. In pottery the Moche excelled in modelled work while their Nazca contemporaries were masters of polychrome painting.

The Spanish conquest had a traumatic effect on the Peruvian Indians. Diseases, particularly smallpox, and the social and economic disruption caused by the collapse of the Inca empire led to a drastic decline in the indigenous population which, according to most estimates, was halved between 1531 and 1561. The biggest drop seems to have been on the coast where whole valleys were reported to have been more or less deserted. It was not until the nineteenth century that the Indian population of Peru showed any significant increase.

The survival of ancient Peru

The majority of the population of present-day Peru has at least some obviously Indian element, such as brown or coppery coloured skins, in its physical appearance. There are relatively few people of pure white Caucasian stock; one reason for this being that the first Spanish conquistadores brought no women with them and had children by Indian women. The type of clothing worn by the Indians is a mixture of indigenous garments, like the poncho worn in the highlands, and clothes derived from central and southern Spain, such as the *sombrero* or straw hat which is now worn in the central and north highlands and on the coast. The modern poncho, basically a cloak with a slit in the top for the head, may have been originally developed by the Araucanian Indians of Chile as a garment for wearing when riding horses. This development took place after the Spanish conquest when they had acquired horses from the Spaniards.

Some traditional forms of architecture like the small house found at Chilca and the pole and estera mat dwellings found on the coast still persist. Also thatching with ichu grass, used in Inca times, is still found in the highlands. Pottery is still being made by traditional moulding and paddle and anvil techniques and fired on open floors and decorated with traditional clay slips. In fact indigenous Indian craft-work is now being officially encouraged to provide goods to sell to tourists and for export. Everything from carved gourds to textiles are being made for both the home and foreign market.

Many of the foods eaten in Peru today are direct descendants of those domesticated several thousand years ago. In particular the varieties of potato and maize are still important staples in the diet both of Indians in the country and urban Peruvians. Mussels and other seafood, whose remains have been found in ancient rubbish heaps all along the coast, are still very much part of the diet of coastal dwellers. The traditional chicha is still a popular drink, particularly in the highlands. Modern soft drinks' technology has produced a fizzy drink called 'Inca Cola' of which only the name bears any relation to Peru's past.

Native religious beliefs and practices with pre-Spanish origins still flourish alongside the official religion, Roman Catholicism. This is especially

Much original stonework survives in the streets of the Inca settlement of Ollantaytambo.

198

true in the mountains, particularly in the south round Cuzco. From 1959 to 1967 Oscar Nuñez del Prado, a Peruvian anthropologist, studied the Quechua Indian village of Kuyo Chico, about 25 kilometres north-east of Cuzco. He found that its inhabitants believed in *Roal*, The Great Spirit Creator, as the universal being who watched over all men and constantly protected them. Roal seems to be very much in the same tradition as Viracocha except that his name is more Spanish-sounding. Roal lives in the high mountain of Ausangate. They also regard many things in nature, such as an old tree, river or rock as having supernatural power and make offerings to them. In addition they carve sacred stone figures or *Illas* to make the crops grow or to get the cattle to breed.

A future for the Peruvian Indians

Peruvian governments are now trying to incorporate the Indians in the national republic since many, being illiterate in Spanish, are excluded from a national franchise. Attempts to teach them to read and write have not always met with success, as typified by a heading in a Lima Sunday newspaper in 1970 which read, in translation: 'They (the Indians) learn to read and write and then they forget'. Efforts are still being made to give the Indians technical help in return for labour on a collective basis rather like in pre-Spanish times. Also the present government has been taking over the haciendas and handing them back to the Indian communities. However, there is still a deep suspicion of governments, a legacy of the more or less continuous exploitation of the Indians by the white ruling classes since the Spanish conquest. The removal of Pizarro's statue from the main square in Lima by the Peruvian government in 1972 and the adoption of Tupac Amaru, an Indian leader who led a rebellion against the Spanish colonial government in the eighteenth century, as a national symbol of Peru's revolution seems to indicate that the Indian population may be more favoured in the coming years.

Further reading

Bennet, W. C. and J. B. Bird, *Andean Culture History* (New York, 1964).

Benson, E. P., *The Mochica: a Culture of Peru* (London, 1972).

Bushnell, G. H. S., *Peru* (London and New York, 1963).

Hemming, J., *The Conquest of the Incas* (London, 1970. Also Abacus paperback, 1972).

Kendall, A., *Everyday Life of the Incas* (London and New York, 1973).

Lanning, E. P., *Peru before the Incas* (Englewood Cliffs, N.J., 1967).

Lathrap, D. W., *The Upper Amazon* (London, 1970).

Moore, S. Falk, *Power and Property in Inca Peru* (New York, 1958).

Moseley, M. E., *The Maritime Foundations of Andean Civilization* (Menlo Park, California, 1975).

Osborne, H., *South American Indian Mythology* (London, 1968).

Willey, G. S., *Introduction to American Archaeology, vol. 2 South America* (Englewood Cliffs, N.J., 1971).

List of illustrations

BLACK AND WHITE PHOTOGRAPHS

116 (bottom) Early Chimú spout and bridge bottle in the form of a woman spinning from a cone of cotton. *c* AD 1000–1200. Museum of the American Indian, Heye Foundation.

120 (top) The fortress of Sacsahuaman, Cuzco. Photo: Elizabeth Kessler.

120 (centre) Inca bronze mace-head from the Upper Amazon area. The Royal Pavilion, Art Gallery and Museums, Brighton. Photo: John Barrow.

120 (bottom) Inca garrison at Tambo Colorado. Photo: Neil Stevenson.

126 (top) Inca aryballus. The Royal Pavilion, Art Gallery and Museums, Brighton. Photo: John Barrow.

126 (bottom) Inca earthenware dish with a bird handle. The Royal Pavilion, Art Gallery and Museums, Brighton. Photo: John Barrow.

127 Machu Picchu. Photo: Victor Kennett.

129 (top) Wooden Inca emblem in the form of a mask. Photo: Michael Holford.

129 (bottom left) Inca skeleton. The Archaeological Museum, Cuzco. Photo: Archive of Elsevier Amsterdam.

129 (bottom right) Inca stone dish. The Archaeological Museum, Cuzco. Photo: Archive of Elsevier Amsterdam.

135 (top) The Black and White Portal and part of the south wing of the Temple of Chavín. Photo: George Bankes.

135 (bottom) Carved, tenoned head in the wall of the Temple of Chavín. Photo: George Bankes.

139 Moche modelled pot in the form of a fanged being fighting a crab. Metropolitan Museum of Art, New York.

140 Moche modelled pot in the form of a fanged being emerging from a mountain-side. Metropolitan Museum of Art, New York.

143 (bottom left) The winter solstice sunset and one of the lines in the desert near Nazca. Photo: Maria Reiche. From *Mystery on the Desert* (1968) by Maria Reiche.

143 (bottom right) Gold ornament with serpent-ended whiskers. From the Nazca Valley. *c* AD 500–750. Museum of the American Indian, Heye Foundation.

151 Chimú stirrup spout bottle in the form of the head of a feline. *c* AD 1200–1470. The Royal Pavilion, Art Gallery and Museums, Brighton. Photo: John Barrow.

155 The Intihuatana Stone at Machu Picchu. Photo: Ewing Galloway N.Y. by courtesy of Aerofilms Ltd.

159 A huaca in modern Peru: the pile of stones marking a significant point at a roadside. Photo: Neil Stevenson.

159 (bottom left and right) A ceremony to ensure the fertility of the herds, taking place on the puna in modern Peru. Photos: Neil Stevenson.

163 The Inca Temple of the Sun at Cuzco surmounted by a Christian church. Photo: George Bankes.

166 (top) Moche bowl, the inside rim painted with looms and weavers. Museum of Mankind, London. Photo: John Barrow.

166 (bottom) Man at work at a backstrap loom today. Photo: Neil Stevenson.

167 (top) Textile with abstract pattern. Völkerkundemuseum, Munich. Photo: Michael Holford.

167 (bottom) Drawing of the pattern of a bird on a fragment of cloth from Huaca Prieta. *c* 2000 BC. From *Preceramic Art from Huaca Prieta, Chicama Valley* (1963) by Junius Bird.

171 (top left) Middle Horizon modelled and painted jar showing a man wearing a textile cap and sleeveless tunic. *c* AD 750–1000. Museum of the American Indian, Heye Foundation.

171 (top centre) Modelled pot in the form of a sandal-shod foot. Probably Inca. Museum of Mankind, London. Photo: John Barrow.

171 (top right) Middle Horizon modelled jar in the form of a man in a pile-weave cap with peaked corners. From Chimbote. *c* AD 500–750. Museum of the American Indian, Heye Foundation.

171 (centre left) Middle Horizon pile-weave cap. From Chimbote. *c* AD 750–1000. Museum of the American Indian, Heye Foundation.

171 (bottom left) Inca sandal from Pachacámac. University Museum, Pennsylvania.

171 (bottom right) Middle Horizon sleeveless tunic of woven alpaca wool. *c* AD 750–1000. Museum of the American Indian, Heye Foundation.

177 (top left) Moche figurine of a man, made in a one-piece mould. *c* AD 200–600. The Royal Pavilion, Art Gallery and Museums, Brighton. Photo: John Barrow.

177 (top right) Nazca polychrome painted bowl. *c* AD 400–600. The Royal Pavilion, Art Gallery and Museums, Brighton. Photo: John Barrow.

Index

metalwork, 182–4; *17–18*, *101*, *180*; pottery, 26, 28, 104, 172; *151*, *179*; religion, 150–3; royal households, 100; social system, 99–109; sodomy, 104; stages of life, 105–7; wars with Pachacámac, 24
Chimú Capac, 34
Chincha, 32, 89
Chongoyape, 138
Chot, 152–3
chronology, 54–6
climate, coastal, 42–4, 45; mountain, 45; Preceramic Period, 56, 58
clothing, 170–5, 197; *171*, *173*
Cobo, Bernabé, 13, 23–4, 157
Collahuayna, 125
Collao, 146
Conchopata, 55, 146, 147
Cordillera Blanca, 132
Corquin, 153
Coslechec, 153
crops, 48–9, 56, 73–4, 75, 79–81
Culebras, 55, 74
La Cumbre, 55, 61
curacas, 100–2, 111
curers, Chimú, 104; Inca, 125–8; Moche, 104
Cuzco, 24, 37, 45, 110, 113, 117–18, 154, 156, 157–8, 161, 162, 184, 186, 193, 199; 'Temple of the Sun', 156, 158–9; *163*

dating methods, 54–7
Day, Kent, 100, 107–9, 190
Desierto, 89
disease, 104, 125–8, 197
divorce, Incas, 121–2
Donnan, Christopher, 94, 175, 186
dress and decorations, 170–5, 197; *171*

earliest men in Peru, 57–8
Early Horizon, 55; definition, 56
Early Intermediate Period, 55; definition, 56
earthquakes, 42, 186
education, Inca, 114–16
Engel, Frederic, 73, 86, 89
environment, coast, 44–5; highlands, 45–7; Pacific Ocean, 42–4; tropical forests, 45, 47
Epigone pottery, 26, 32
Espinosa, Antonio Vázquez de, 132
Estete, Miguel de, 10–12, 24, 27
Evans, Clifford, 92, 94, 132

farming, *see* agriculture
Farrington, Ian, 76
fishing, 42, 68–73, 89; *67*
food, contemporary Indian, 197; fishing, 42, 68–73; *67*; gathering, 68; hunting, 56, 57, 61–8, 86; *see also* agriculture

Galinat, W. C., 73
Gallinazo, 75
graves, *see* burials
Grosse, Charlotte, 29, 33, 37
Grosse, Johannes, 29
guano, 42; *43*

Hacienda Ocucaje, 32
Hampi, Camayoc, 125
Hanan Cuzco, 110
head deformation, 48, 138
Hearst, Phoebe, 29, 33, 34, 37

houses, 186–7, 195, 197; *183*
Huaca Chotuna, 153
Huaca de la Cruz, 94
Huaca de la Luna, 30–2, 92, 187
Huaca de Los Reyes, 138
Huaca del Sol, 30–2, 92, 187, 190; *8*, *185*
Huaca el Brujo, *59*
Huaca Negra, 71, 132
Huaca Prieta, 55, 71, 74
huacas, 60, 152, 157–8
Huacho Valley, 24
Huaitará, 33
Huamachuco, 32
Huamán, 153
Huamán Valley, 24
Huanacauri, 158
Huancaco, 187
Huanachaco, 72
Huarachico, 117–18
Huaral Viejo, 34
Huari, 55, 56, 147–50
Huascarán, 42
Huayna Capac, 122, 157
Huayurco, 83
Humboldt, Alexander von, 42
Humboldt Current, 42, 68
hunting, 56, 57, 61–8, 86
Hurin Cuzco, 110–11

Ica, 55
Ica Valley, 32, 54, 74, 89; *77*
Inca, 55; achievement, 196; age groups, 110; agriculture, 79–81; *70*; architecture, 193–5; *194*; children, 113–14; *115*; clothing, 172–5; *173*; dominance of Peru, 54; education, 114–16; geographical models, 76; hunting, 66; language, 48; legal system, 111–13; life cycle, 113–30; marriage, 110, 119–22; measurement of time, 113; medicine, 125–8; metalwork, 182, 184; pottery, 22, 37; *128*; puberty, 117; records of numbers, 85; *84*; religion, 153–64; roads, 85; rulers and government, 110–11; social organization, 109–13; sodomy, 104, 112; taxes and tributes, 72, 111, 121, 122; trade, 83–5
Indians, contemporary, 47–8, 197–9; *192*
Initial Period, 55; definition, 56
irrigation, 44, 74–9, 92, 144

Janaq Pacha, 164
Jequetepeque, 76
Jívaro, 37

Kalasasaya, 144
Kauri, 138–41
Kosok, Paul, 142–4
Kotosh, 55, 132
Kroeber, 32
Kuismanqu, 24
Kuntur Wasi, 138
Kuyo Chico, 199

Lambayeque Valley, 100, 138, 181
languages, Chimú, 48, 100; Inca, 48; Moche, 60; at Pachacámac, 23–4
Lanning, Edward P., 54, 56, 58, 68, 71
Lanzón, 134, 136; *137*
Larco Hoyle, Rafael, 60, 83, 141, 150, 186
Late Horizon, 55; definition, 54